THE CULT

CEREMONY

THE CULT

CEREMONY

OFF THE RECORD

Folio © 1992 Warner Chappell Music Ltd
129 Park Street, London W1Y 3FA
Music Transcribed by Barnes Music Engraving Ltd, East Sussex TN22 4HA
Designed and Printed by Panda Press, Haverhill, Suffolk

Magic in Rituals of Rock

The Cult's 'Ceremony' album celebrates tribal spirituality

The Cult's Ian Astbury sees a rock concert as "a ceremony, a gathering, a place where you can dress up, you can put your tribal colours on (and) come into a space which is created purely for one event."

And that's the basis of the British band's new album, "Ceremony."

Throughout the record, Astbury urges listeners to consider the need for what he calls "ritual space," as he explained in a telephone interview:

Why We Need It

"We need ritual space in life to discuss and express ourselves. People aren't aware of these spaces as being important. We live in a world (and) it's an organic thing; there is a metaphysical aspect to life. People are so far removed from that.

"Once you get into a true self, a spiritual nature, then you begin to articulate yourself in the real world. Your quality of life is improved, you feel more confident about yourself, you feel more contented within yourself."

"That's all part of ritual space, being aware of that, and I think one of the last ritual spaces we have, especially for young people, is a live concert."

Important Visit

Astbury's interest in things mystical stems from a visit at age 12 to an Indian reservation, while he was living in Canada.

"I was just fascinated with the fact that here (was) an indigenous people in its own environment," he said. "I had never seen tribal peoples, and they were human beings — they weren't being chased across the movie screen by John Wayne—but their culture was so radically different from mine. I wanted to know what it was all about.

"It wasn't a romantic thing. It was the fact that they had a relationship with the Earth that we didn't have, that we should have."

Seeking Purity

Astbury's interest in a more basic, earth-conscious culture seeps through "Ceremony" in songs such as "Earth Mofo" and the title track. In the stream-of-consciousness lyrics of "White," Astbury longs for a purity of life he feels is missing from society.

The sparsely orchestrated "Indian" pairs a mournful cello with the acoustic guitar of Billy Duffy. The Indian woman of the lyrics, Astbury said, serves as a metaphor for many things, including his relationship with the Earth and the tragically lost Indian way of life.

"Ceremony" is without some of the blustery male posturing that marked songs like "Sun King" and "Fire Woman" on 1989's "Sonic Temple."

Both Sides

"I've always said and I always will say that sensitivity is a strength, not a weakness, not only as a writer, but as a human being," he said. "You've gotta have rhythm and you've gotta have melody, you've gotta have conscious and subconscious activity, you've gotta have feminine and masculine (sides). You've gotta have both sides and be in control of both sides."

Astbury said "Ceremony" surpasses its predecessor because of its emphasis on rhythm, partially brought about by the departure of longtime bassist Jamie Stewart and drummer Matt Sorum, now with Guns N' Roses, and the addition of two new members.

Charlie Drayton replaced Stewart, and Mickey Curry replaced Sorum on the album, but they're not part of the band's current tour. Curry played on "Sonic Temple," and Astbury chose Drayton after being impressed by his work on Keith Richards' 1988 solo tour.

Duffy, a constant in the band since its beginning as Southern Death Cult in 1983, seems also to have caught on to rhythm. He still breaks into solos, but they're not the main focus of the song's guitar base—that's left to the rhythm line.

Astbury carries his mysticism into the way he dresses, especially onstage. He's been interested in clothes since he was a youngster in England.

"I think clothes really reflect the time and the environment and your headspace as well," he said. "I dress to kill then I perform—I dress to kill in ritual space."

`Soul Scars'

Even tattoos carry their own mystique for Astbury.

"Some people have got big tattoos because they want to be big men," he said. "I've got four – all my tattoos represent something to me. I call them soul scars, because that's what they are to me. "I still view the world in a ritual, tribalistic kind of way, so all my symbolism and words and the way I dress, my hair (it's long, straight, and jet black), my tattoos and everything really reflect a lifestyle that I live by, a code that I live by daily."

THE
CULT

THE
CULT

CEREMONY

OFF THE RECORD

Notation and Tablature Explained

Open C chord

Scale of E major

High E (1st) string
B (2nd) string
G (3rd) string
D (4th) string
A (5th) string
Low E (6th) string

Bent Notes:

The note fretted is always shown first. Variations in pitch achieved by string bending are enclosed within this symbol ⌐ ¬ . If you aren't sure how far to bend the string, playing the notes indicated without bending gives a guide to the pitches to aim for. The following examples cover the most common string bending techniques:

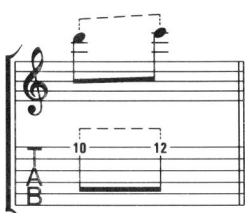

Example 1:
Play the D, bend up one tone (two half-steps) to E.

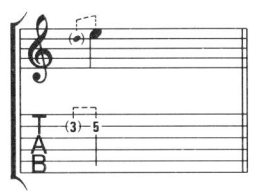

Example 4:
Pre-bend: fret the D, bend up one tone to E, then pick.

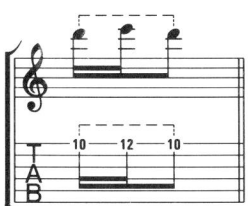

Example 2:
Play the D, bend up one tone to E then release bend to sound D. Only the first note is picked.

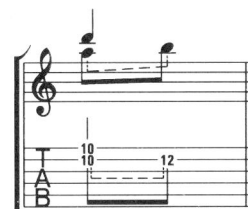

Example 5:
Play the A and D together, then bend the B-string up one tone to sound B.

Example 3: Fast bend: Play the D, then bend up one tone to E as quickly as possible.

Example 6:
Play the D and F♯ together, then bend the G-string up one tone to E, and the B-string up ½ tone to G.

Additional guitaristic techniques have been notated as follows:

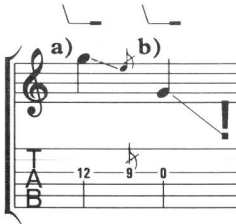

Tremolo Bar:
Alter pitch using tremolo bar. Where possible, the pitch to aim for is shown.
a) Play the G; use the bar to drop the pitch to E.
b) Play the open G; use the bar to 'divebomb', i.e. drop the pitch as far as possible.

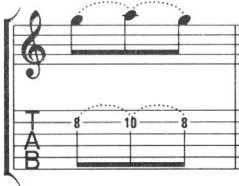

Hammer on and Pull off:
Play first note, sound next note by 'hammering on', the next by 'pulling off'. Only the first note is picked.

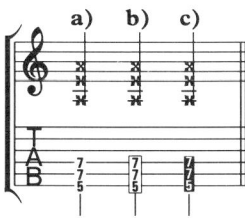

Mutes:
a) Right hand mute:
Mute strings by resting the right hand on the strings just above the bridge.
b) Left hand mute:
Damp the strings by releasing left hand pressure just after the notes sound.
c) Unpitched mute:
Damp the strings with the left hand to produce a percussive sound.

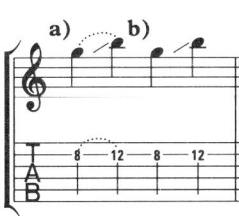

Glissando:
a) Play first note, sound next note by sliding up string. Only the first note is picked.
b) As above, but pick second note.

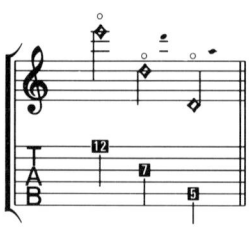

Natural Harmonics:
Touch the string over the fret marked and pick to produce a bell-like tone. The small notes show the resultant pitch, where necessary.

Vibrato:
Apply vibrato, by 'shaking' note or with tremolo bar. As vibrato is so much a matter of personal taste and technique, it is indicated only where essential.

Artificial Harmonics:
Fret the lowest note, touch string over fret indicated by diamond notehead and pick. Small notes show the resultant pitch.

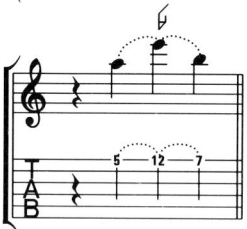

Tapping:
Sound notes indicated by tapping – hammering-on with the picking hand at the indicated fret.

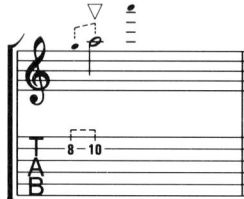

Pinch Harmonics:
Fret the note as usual, but 'pinch' or 'squeeze' the string with the picking hand to produce a harmonic overtone. Small notes show the resultant pitch.

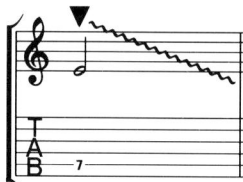

Pick Scratch:
Scrape the pick down the strings – this works best on the wound strings.

Quarter-tones:
A downwards arrow means the written pitch is lowered by a quarter-tone; an upwards arrow raises the written pitch by a quarter-tone.

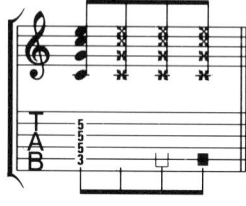

Repeated Chords:
To make rhythm guitar parts easier to read the tablature numbers may be omitted when a chord is repeated. The example shows a C major chord played naturally, r/h muted, l/h muted and as an unpitched mute respectively.

Special Tunings:
Non-standard tunings are shown as 'tuning boxes'. Each box represents one guitar string, the leftmost box corresponding to the lowest pitched string. The symbol '•' in a box means the pitch of the corresponding string is not altered. A note within a box means the string must be re-tuned as stated. For tablature readers, numbers appear in the boxes. The numbers represent the number of half-steps the string must be tuned up or down. The tablature relates to an instrument tuned as stated.

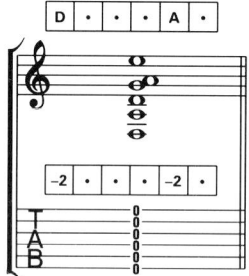

Tune the low E (6th) string down one tone (two half-steps) to D. Tune the B (2nd) string down one tone (two half-steps) to A.
See 'White'.

Chord naming:

The following chord naming convention has been used. Note that chord symbols show the overall harmony, sometimes simplified, and are not intended to indicate a suitable accompaniment. Altered 5ths are shown as 'dim5' or 'aug5', whilst alterations to added notes are indicated by '#' or '♭'.

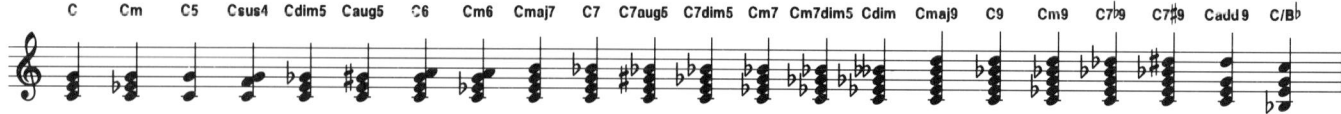

Where there is no appropriate chord symbol, for example when the music consists of a repeated figure (or riff) the tonal base is indicated in parenthesis:

Key to Percussion Notation

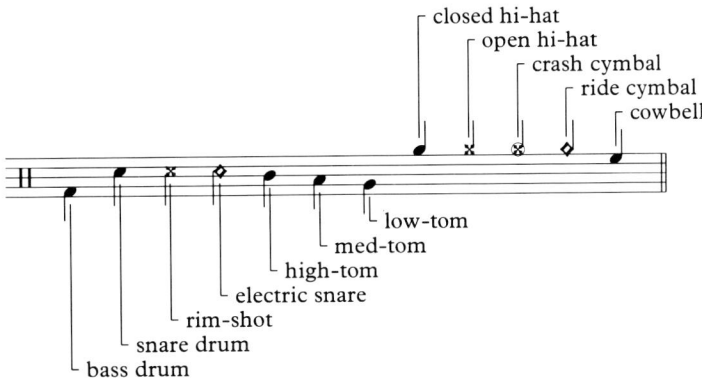

Specific percussion techniques:

 Cymbal muted by hand.

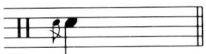 Flam: two hits in rapid succession.

 Hit with both sticks at the same time.

 Open/closed hi-hat, i.e. hit open hi-hat with stick, close with pedal.

Ceremony

Words & Music by
Ian Astbury and Billy Duffy

Kbd. 1
Kbd. 2
Kbd. 3
(8vb)
Perc.
Perc.

0:19
Gtr. 1
Gtr. 1 Tab.
Kbd. 1
Kbd. 2
Kbd. 3
(8vb)
Perc.
Perc.

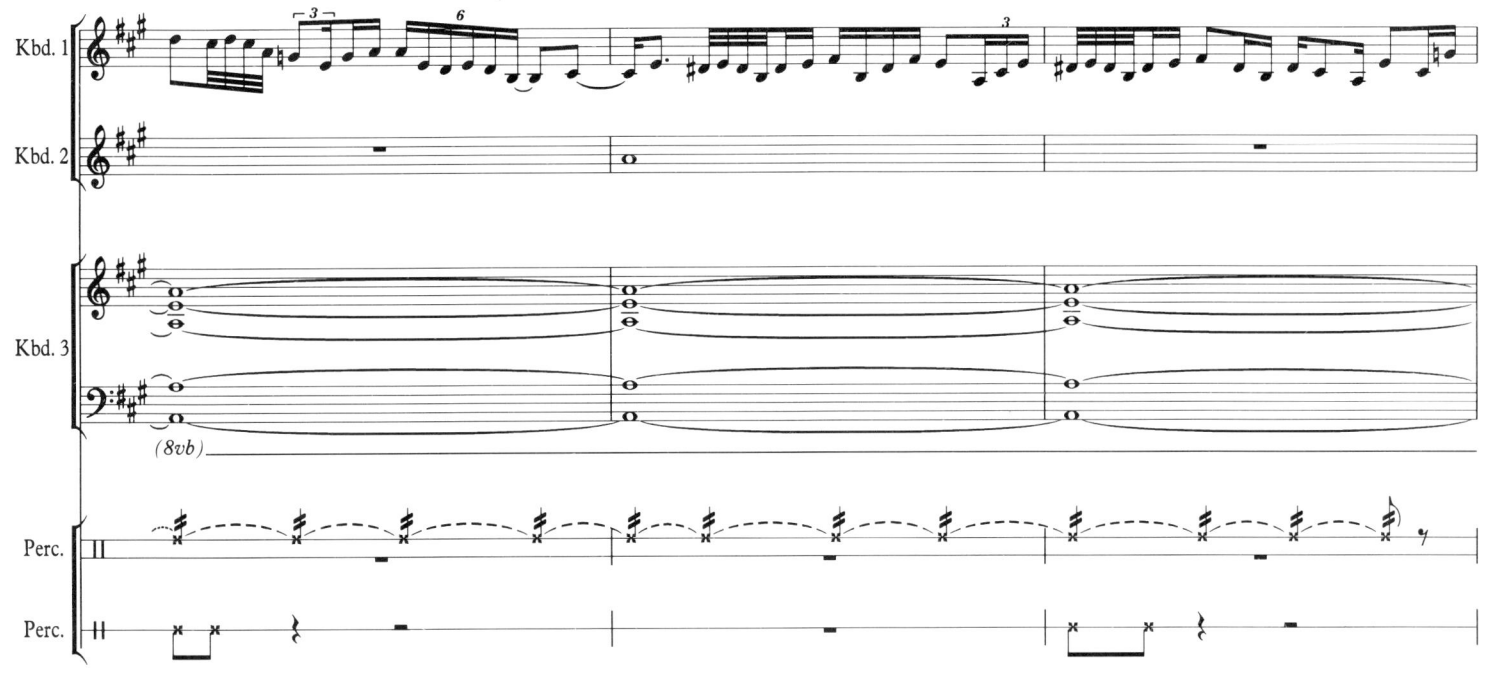

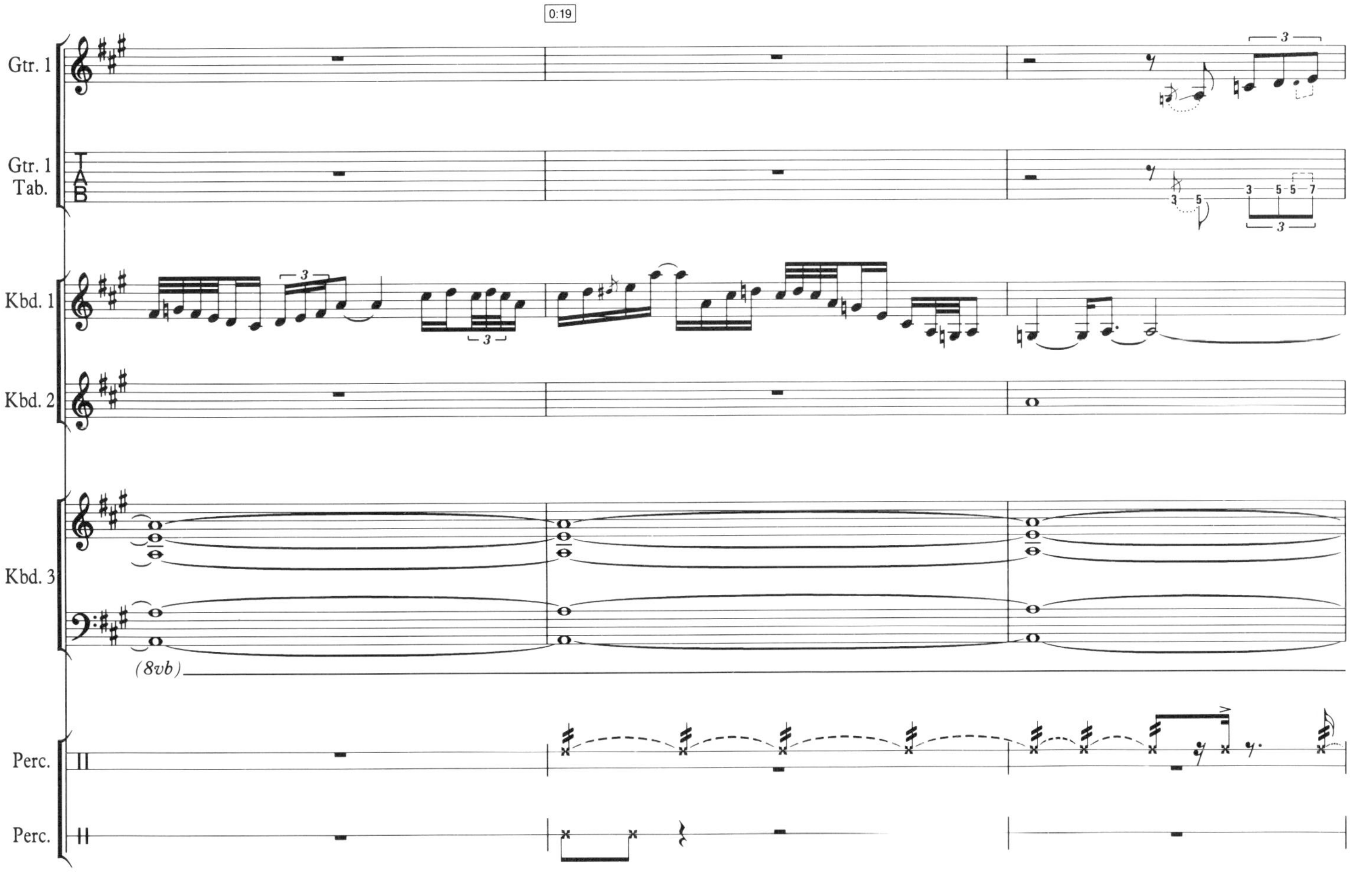

Gtr. 1
Gtr. 1 Tab.
Kbd. 1
Kbd. 3
(8vb)
Bs.
Bs. Tab.
Perc.
Maracas
Perc.
Dr.
Gtr. 1
Gtr. 1 Tab.
Kbd. 3
(8vb)
let ring
Bs.
Bs. Tab.
Perc.
Perc.
Dr.

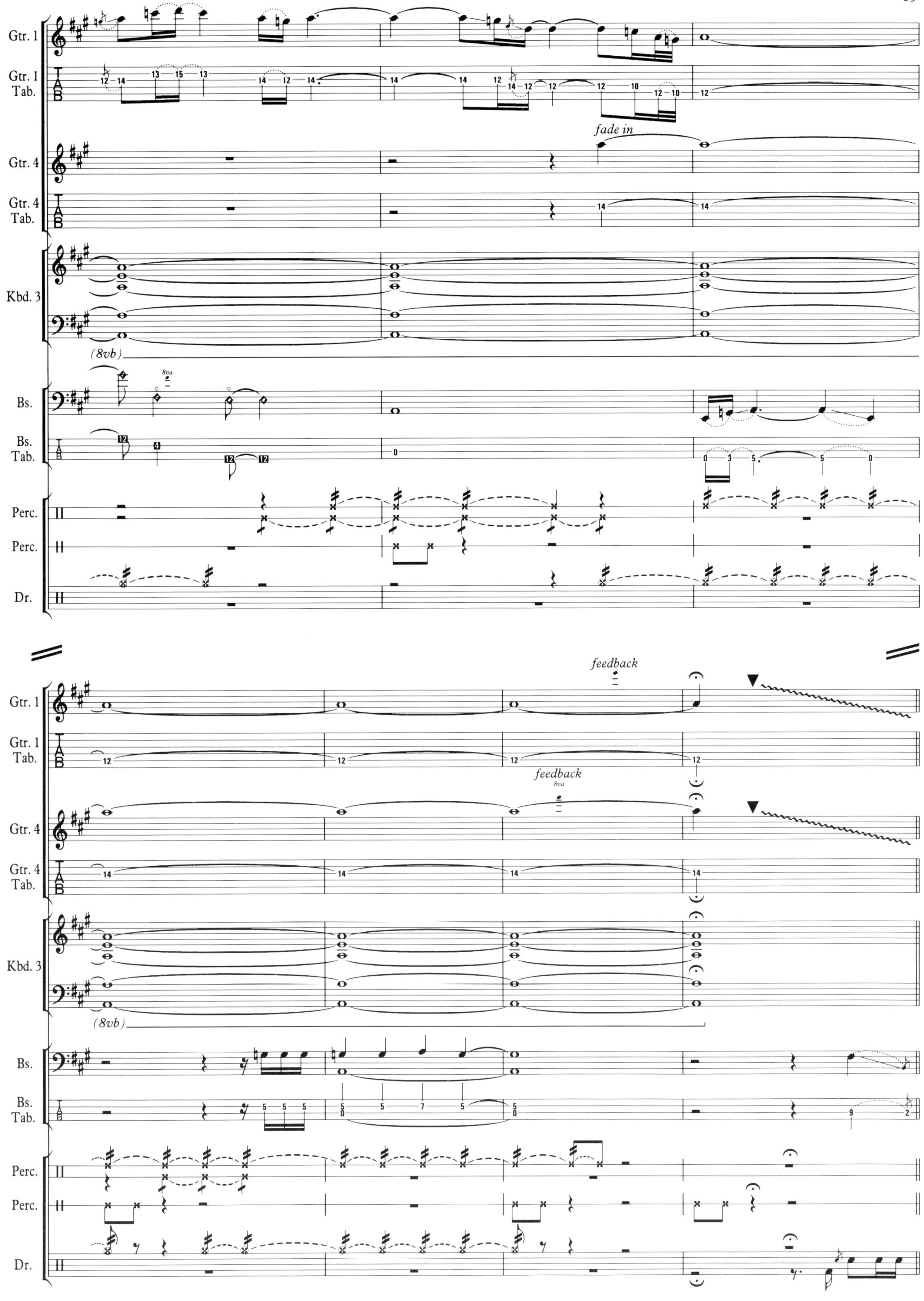
Gtr. 1
Gtr. 1 Tab.
Gtr. 4
Gtr. 4 Tab.
Kbd. 3
(8vb)
Bs.
Bs. Tab.
Perc.
Perc.
Dr.
fade in
feedback
feedback
8va

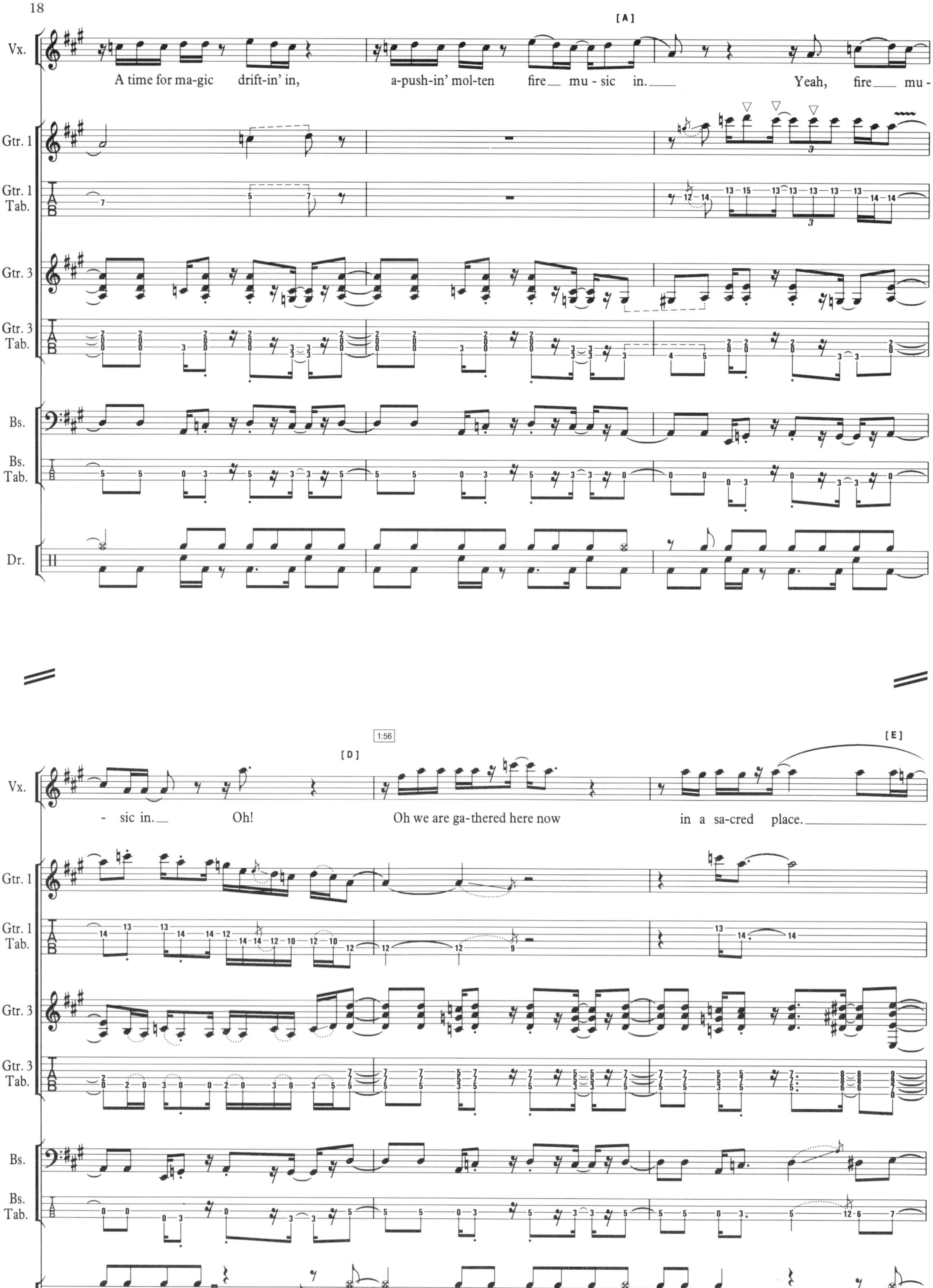
[A]
Vx.
A time for ma-gic drift-in' in, a-push-in' mol-ten fire mu-sic in. Yeah, fire mu-
Gtr. 1
Gtr. 1 Tab.
Gtr. 3
Gtr. 3 Tab.
Bs.
Bs. Tab.
Dr.
1:56
[D]
[E]
-sic in. Oh! Oh we are ga-thered here now in a sa-cred place.

Ce-re-mo - ny. Funk-y style mu-sic got you good now child-ren. Ce-re-mo - ny. A-

- rock 'n' roll mu-sic got you good. Oh! An-cient rhy-thm hit ma-chine. Oh ri-tual mu-sic flow-ing strong and free.

Flow-ing strong and free.

A ce-le-bra-tion that we need___

Flow-ing strong and free.

8va

to cleanse a world that is bleed-ing deep.

Ooh no no___ bleed___ no!

[4:23]

[A]

Vx.

A - funk-y style mu-sic got you good,   good, good.   Ce-re-mo - ny.   A -

B. Vx.

Ce - re-mo - ny.   Ce - re-mo -

Gtr. 1

(8va)   8va

Gtr. 1 Tab.

20   14   13 15 13 15-13 14   14   14.   15-17

Guitar 4 doubles

Gtr. 3

Gtr. 3 Tab.

Bs.

Bs. Tab.

Perc.

Dr.

- rock 'n' roll mu-sic got you good   ba - by.   Ce-re-mo - ny.   A ce-re - mo - ny,   got   you good yeah!

B. Vx.

- ny.   Ce - re-mo - ny.

Gtr. 1

(8va)

Gtr. 1 Tab.

17   12-14 13-15-13-15 15-13 14   14   12-14-12   11-12 11.   9-10 9 10-9 10-9 10-9-10

Vx.
Oh!
Ce - re-mo - ny.
Gtr. 1
Gtr. 1 Tab.
Gtr. 3
Gtr. 3 Tab.
Bs.
Bs. Tab.
Perc.
Dr.
5:11
[D]
Come on!

Wild Hearted Son

Words & Music by
Ian Astbury and Billy Duffy

Well now!

40

42

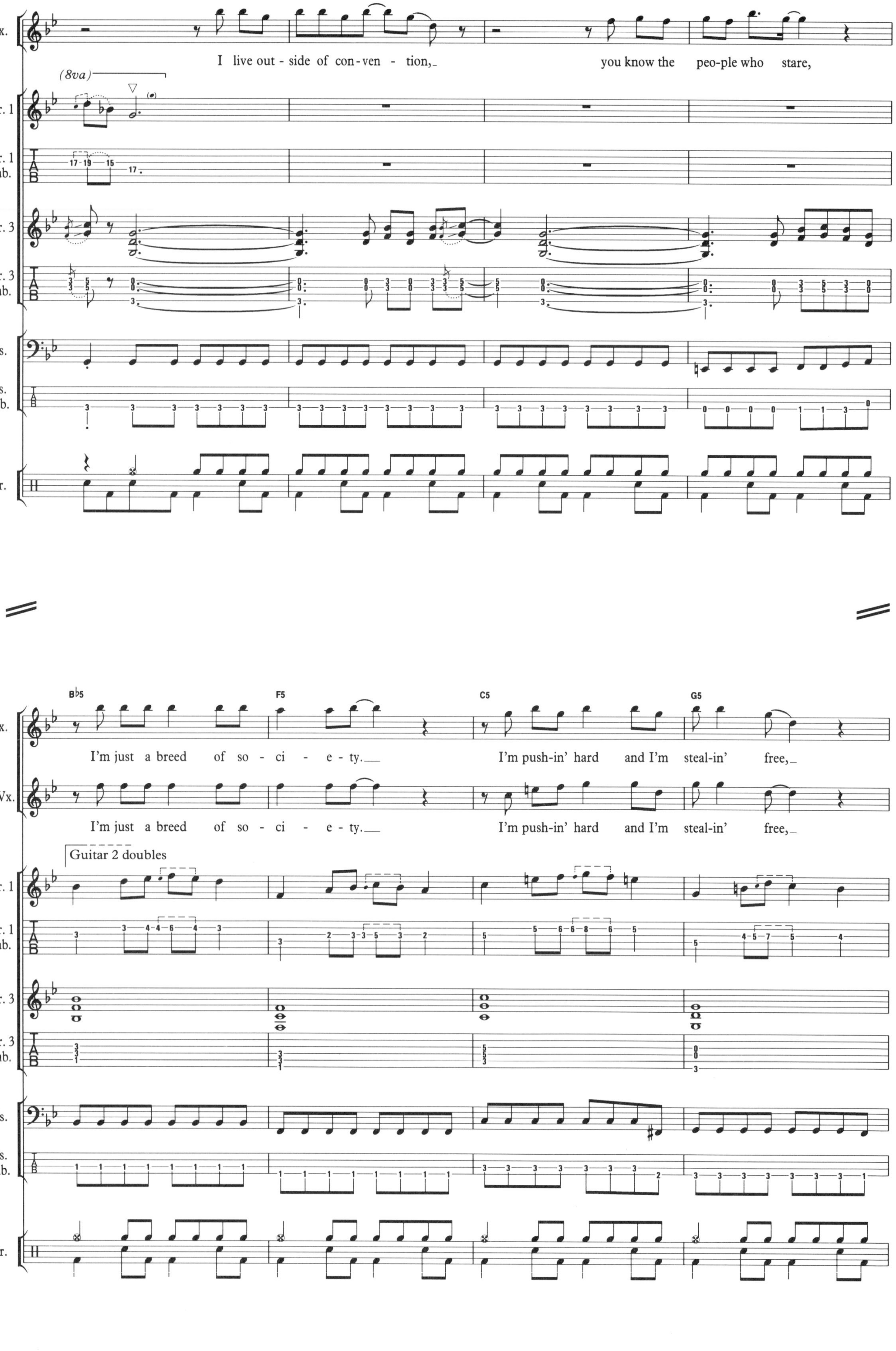
Vx.
I live out - side of con - ven - tion, you know the peo - ple who stare,
(8va)
Gtr. 1
Gtr. 1 Tab.
Gtr. 3
Gtr. 3 Tab.
Bs.
Bs. Tab.
Dr.
B♭5
F5
C5
G5
Vx.
I'm just a breed of so - ci - e - ty. I'm push-in' hard and I'm steal-in' free,
B. Vx.
I'm just a breed of so - ci - e - ty. I'm push-in' hard and I'm steal-in' free,
Guitar 2 doubles
Gtr. 1
Gtr. 1 Tab.
Gtr. 3
Gtr. 3 Tab.
Bs.
Bs. Tab.
Dr.

Vx.
C
G
B♭5
C5
wild heart - ed son.
Wild heart-ed
(8va)
Gtr. 1
Gtr. 1 Tab.
Gtr. 3
Gtr. 3 Tab.
Bs.
Bs. Tab.
Perc.
Dr.
5:09
Dmadd9
G7/F
Cadd9
G
son,
the
8va
Gtr. 2
Gtr. 2 Tab.
12-str. Gtr.
12-str. Gtr. Tab.
Kbd. 2
+ 8vb

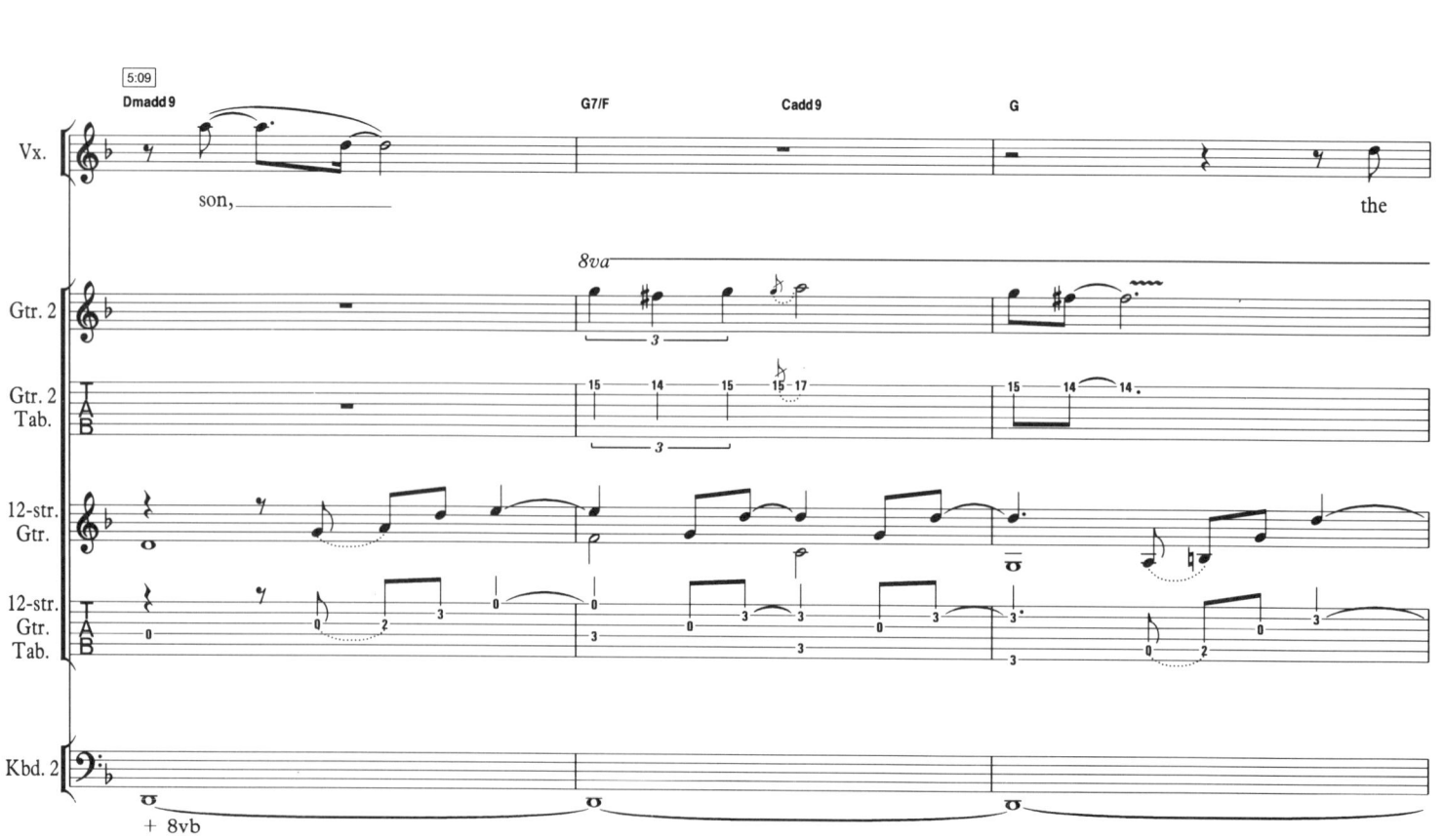

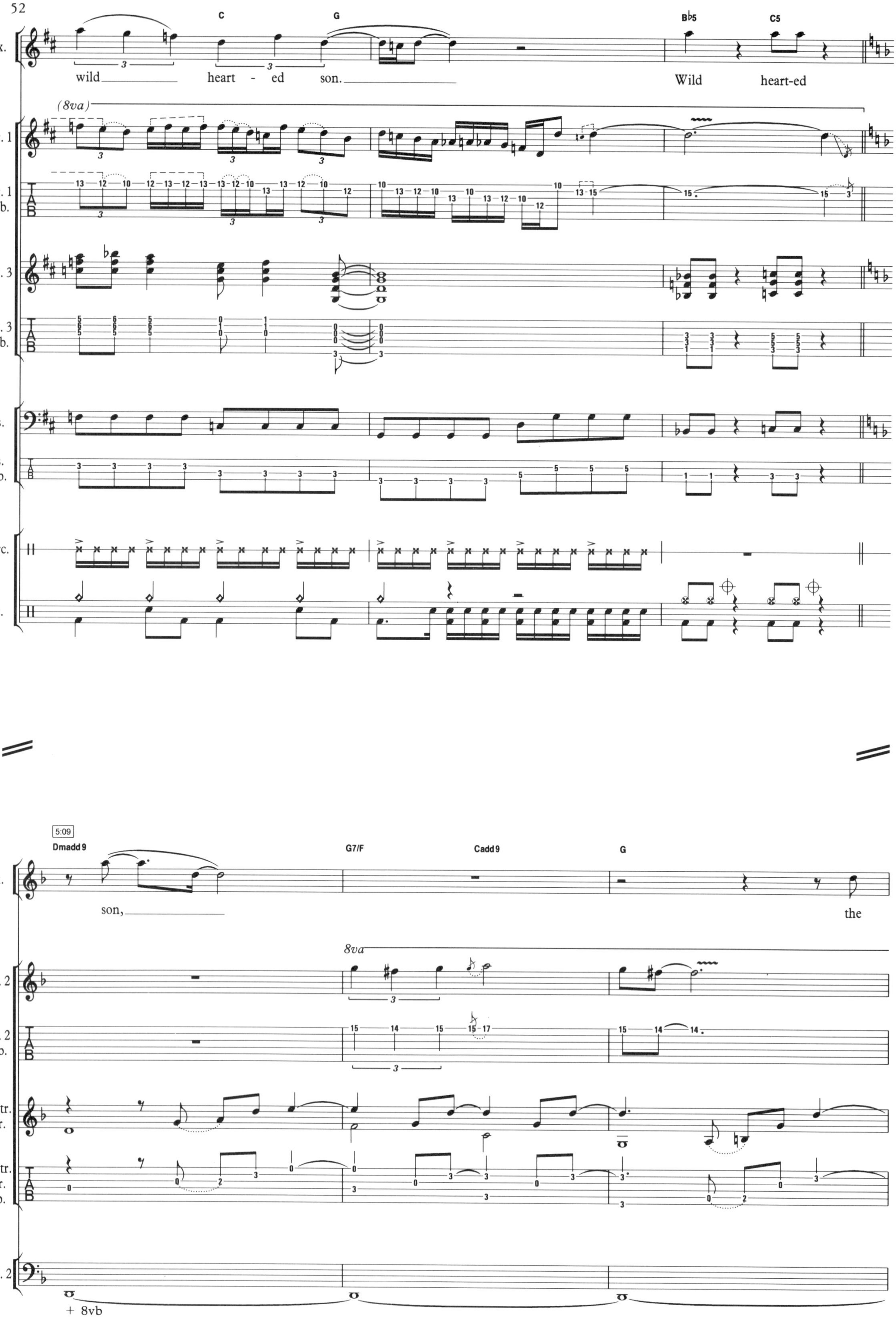

53

world did-n't want you to run.

I'm a wild

heart-ed son.

Earth Mofo

Words & Music by
Ian Astbury and Billy Duffy

56

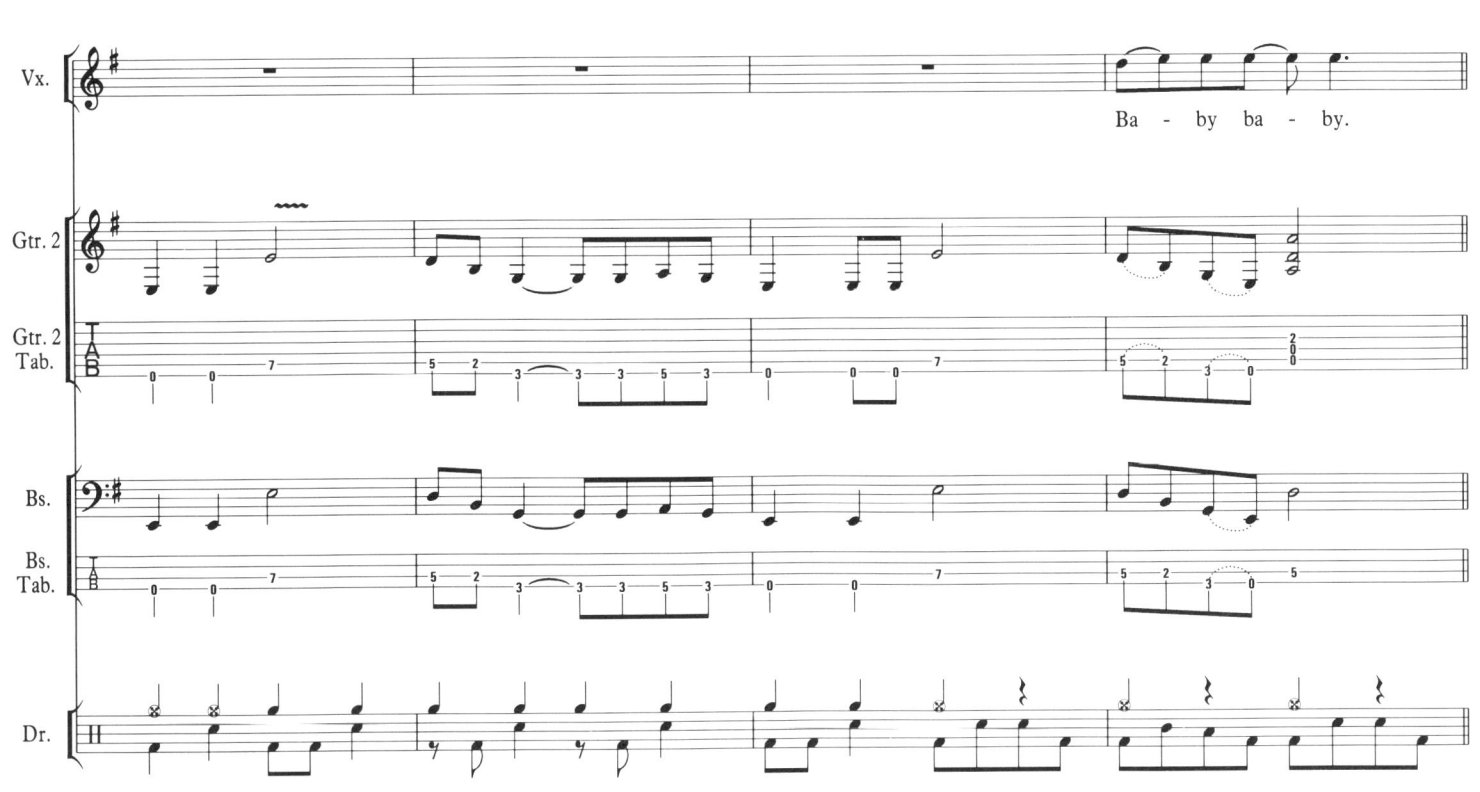

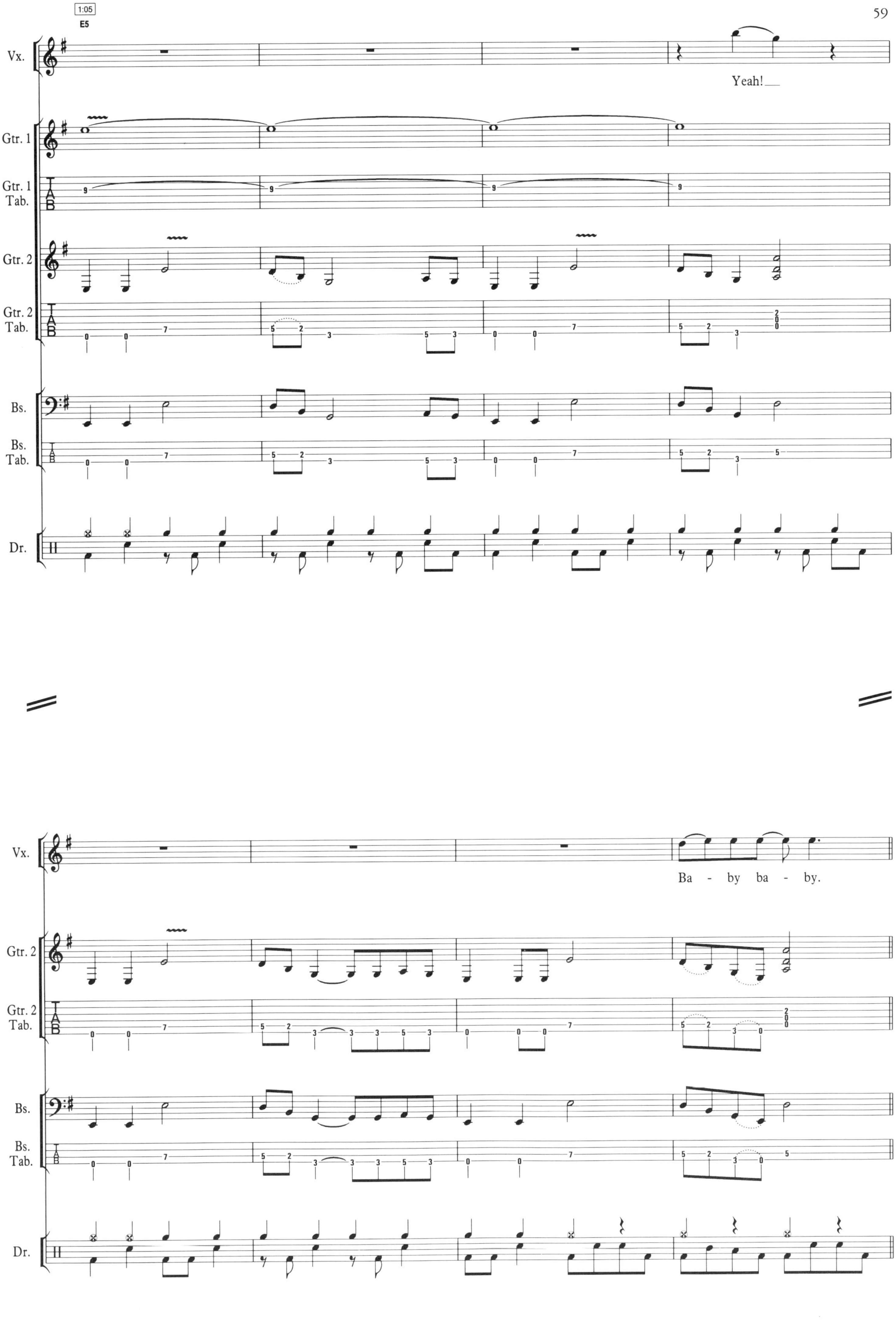
1:05
E5
Vx.
Yeah!
Gtr. 1
Gtr. 1 Tab.
Gtr. 2
Gtr. 2 Tab.
Bs.
Bs. Tab.
Dr.
Vx.
Ba - by ba - by.
Gtr. 2
Gtr. 2 Tab.
Bs.
Bs. Tab.
Dr.

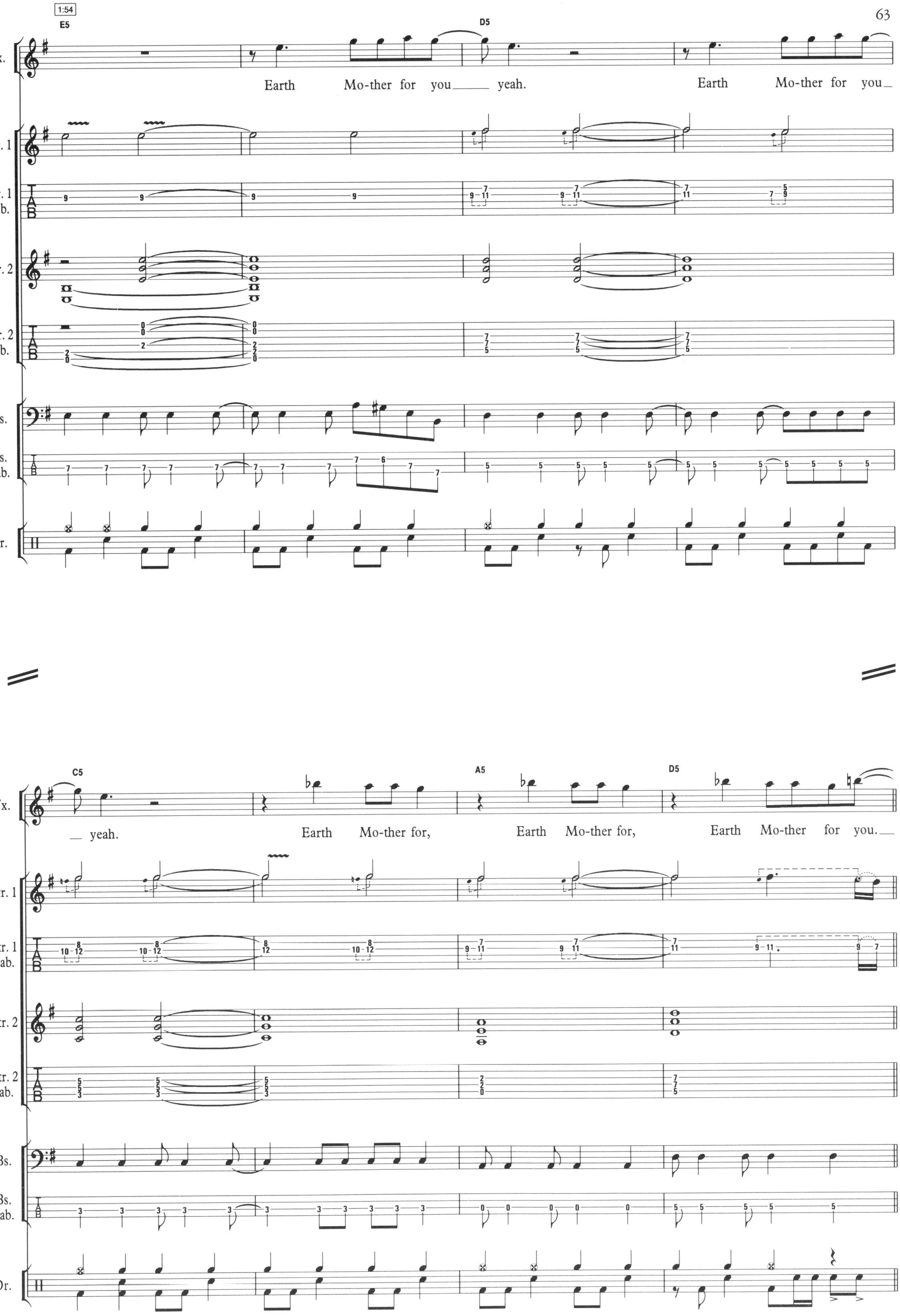
1:54
E5
D5
Vx.
Earth Mo-ther for you___ yeah. Earth Mo-ther for you_
Gtr. 1
Gtr. 1 Tab.
Gtr. 2
Gtr. 2 Tab.
Bs.
Bs. Tab.
Dr.
C5
A5
D5
_ yeah. Earth Mo-ther for, Earth Mo-ther for, Earth Mo-ther for you.__

2:04
[E]
Vx.
Wow!
Gtr. 1
Gtr. 1 Tab.
Gtr. 2
Gtr. 2 Tab.
Bs.
Bs. Tab.
Dr.
Vx.
Well lis - ten.
feedback
Gtr. 1
Gtr. 1 Tab.
Gtr. 2
Gtr. 2 Tab.
Bs.
Bs. Tab.
Dr.

What do you want? What do you want? What do you... What do you want___ now? Think a-bout it.

What do you want? What do you want? What do you... What do you want now?

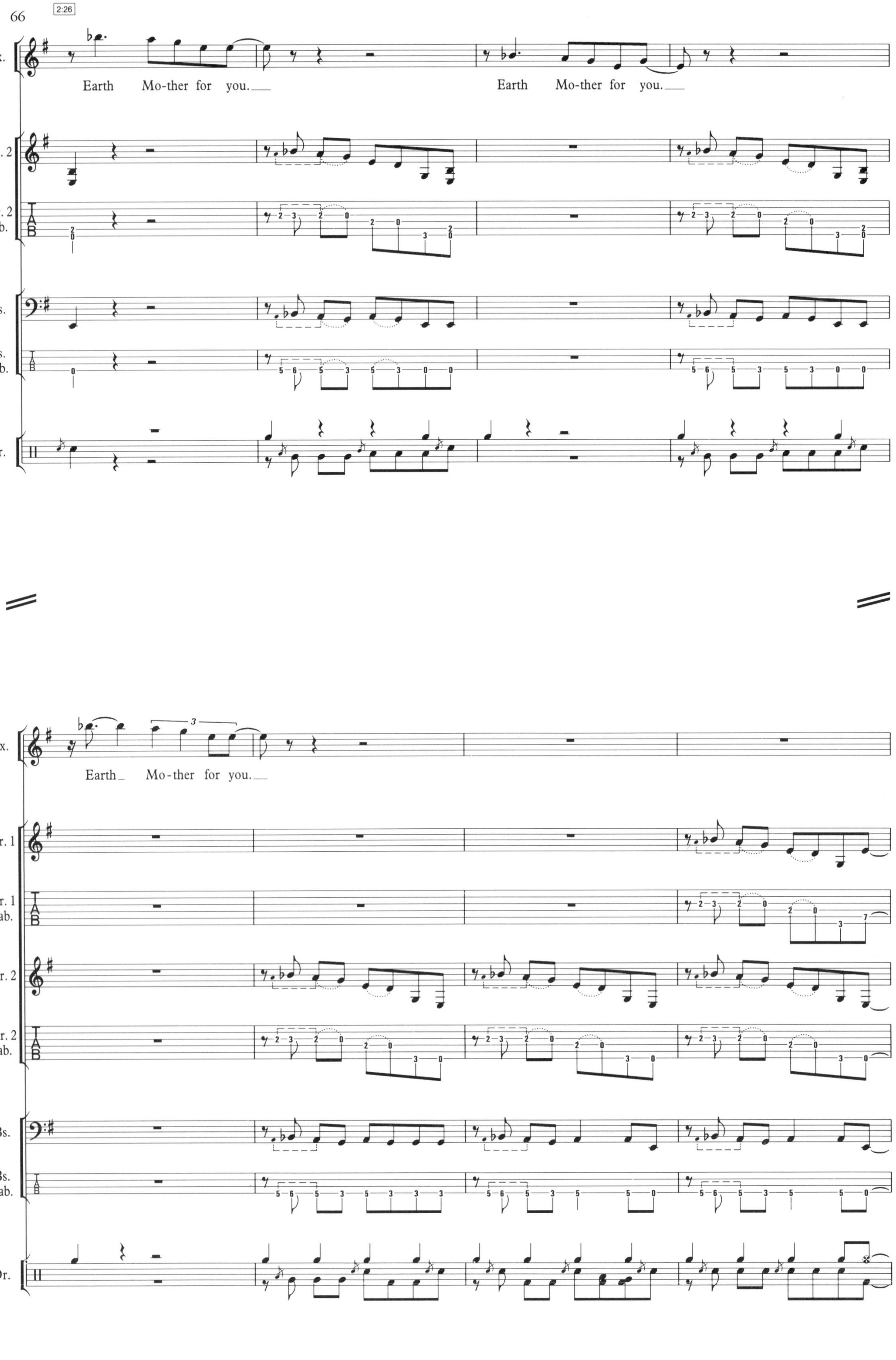

Earth   Mo-ther for you.____   Earth   Mo-ther for you.____

Earth__ Mo-ther for you.____

68

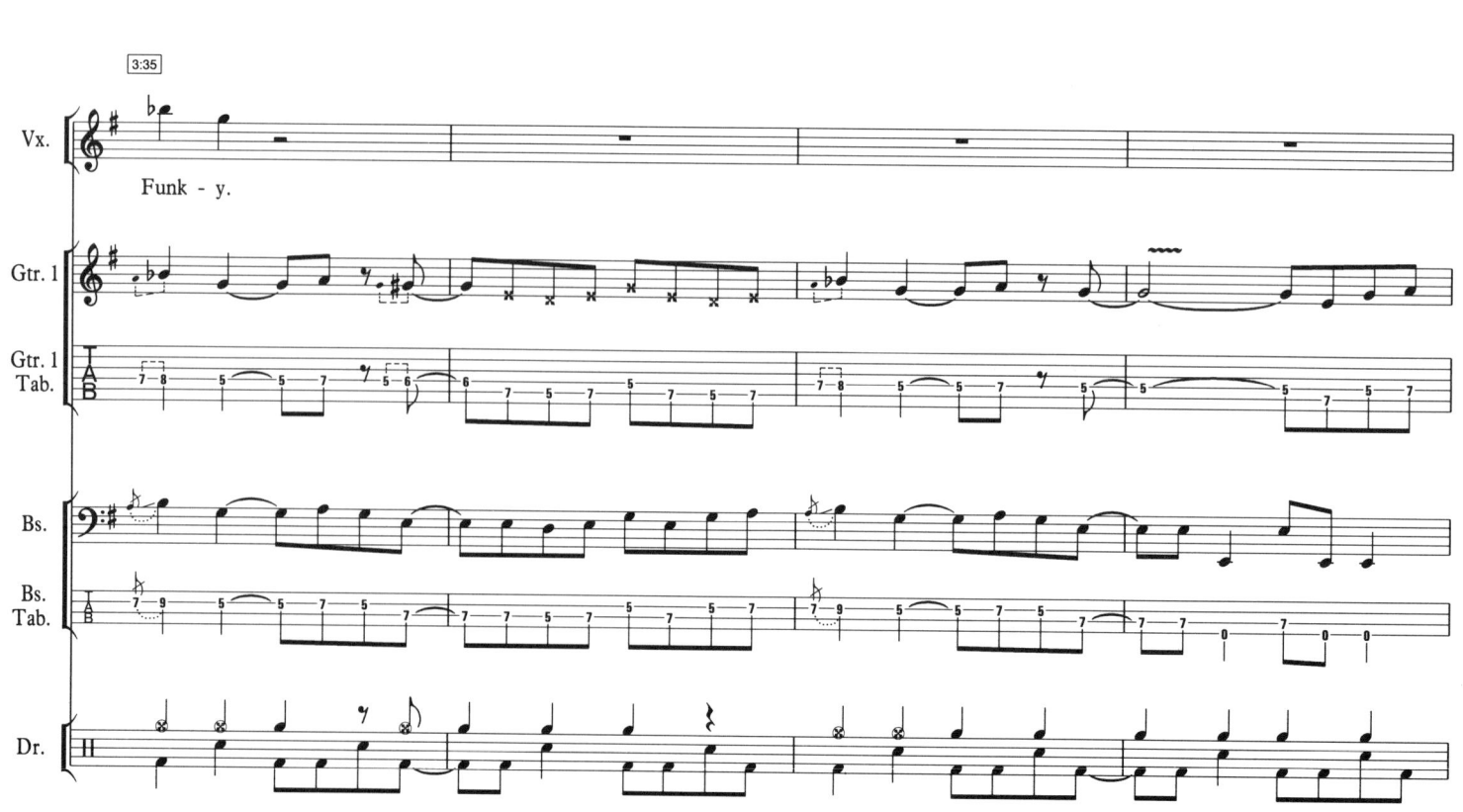

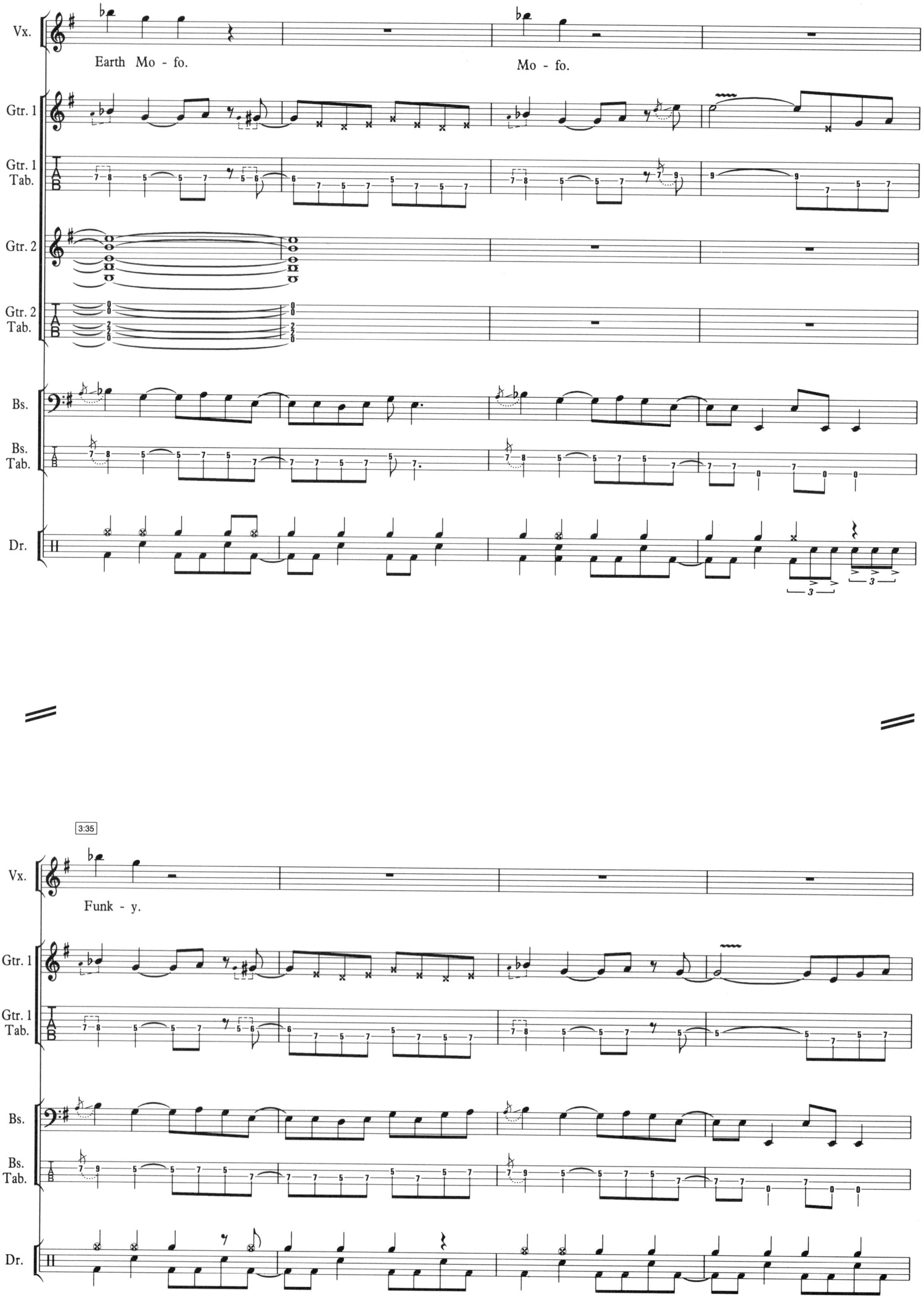
Vx.
Earth Mo - fo.
Mo - fo.
Gtr. 1
Gtr. 1 Tab.
Gtr. 2
Gtr. 2 Tab.
Bs.
Bs. Tab.
Dr.
3:35
Funk - y.

Free time

Vx. Earth Mo-ther for you._____ Yeah._____

Yeah yeah yeah_____ yeah. Wow yeah.

8va

feedback

ad lib.

White

Words & Music by
Ian Astbury and Billy Duffy

(8va)
0:40
Ac. Gtr. 1
Ac. Gtr. 1 Tab.
Ac. Gtr. 2
Acoustic Guitar 3 doubles
Ac. Gtr. 2 Tab.
Ac. Gtr. 3
Ac. Gtr. 3 Tab.
Bs.
Bs. Tab.

Ac. Gtr. 2
Ac. Gtr. 2 Tab.
Dr.

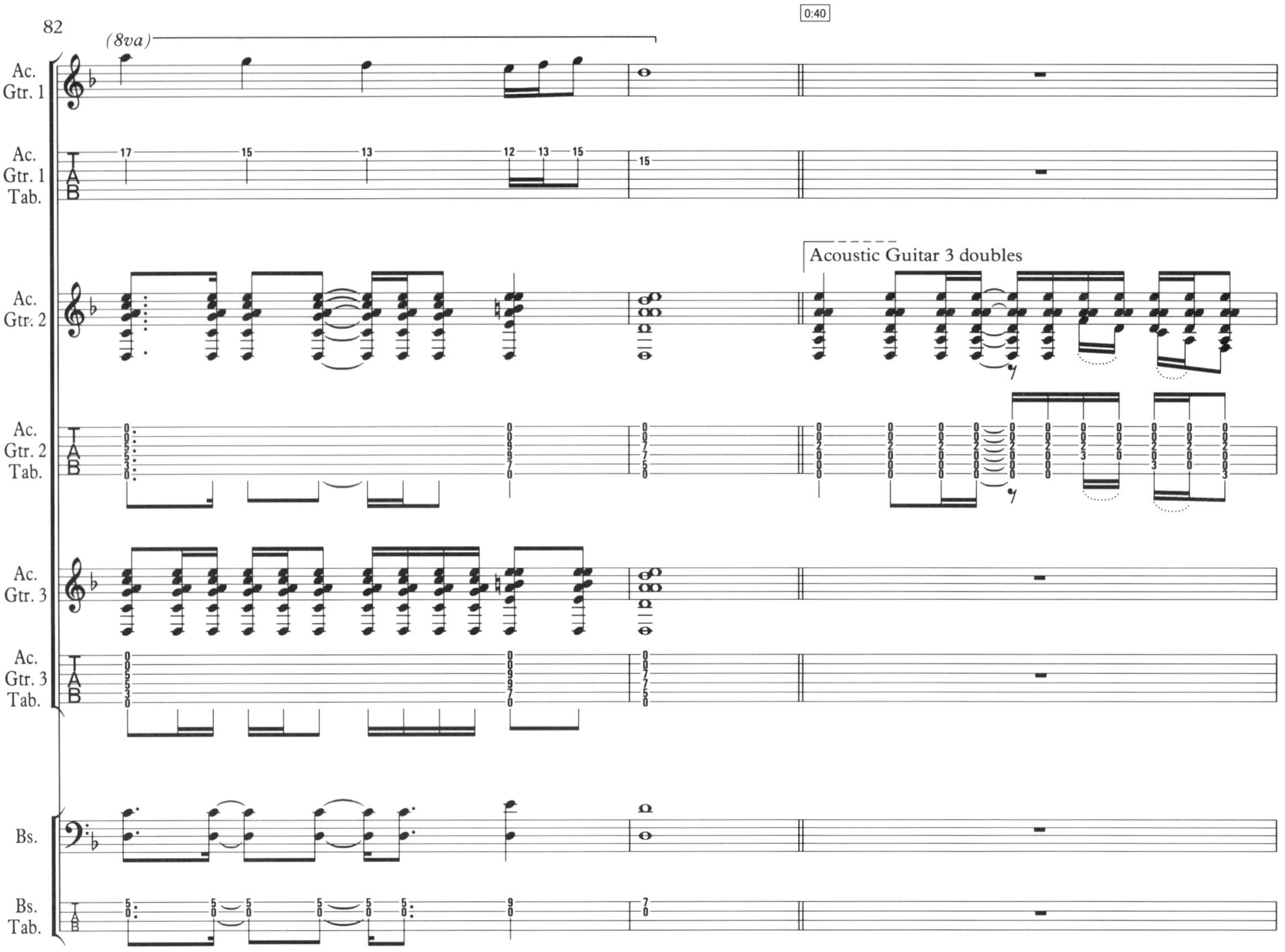

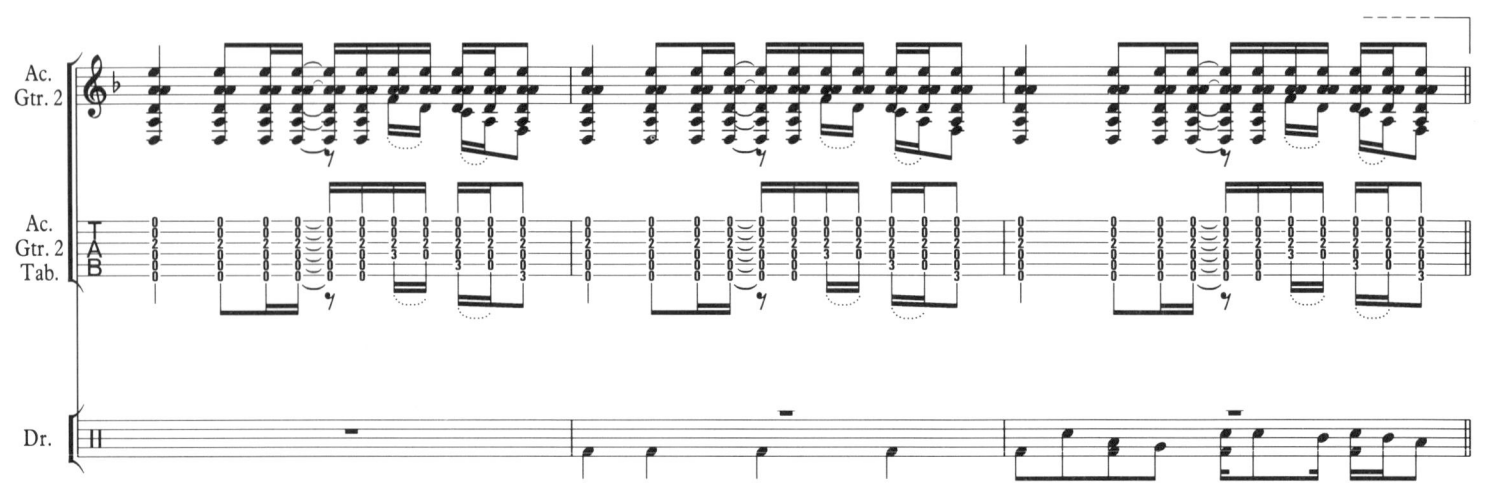

83

84

shin-ing   bright - ly.   White,_____   yeah   white,

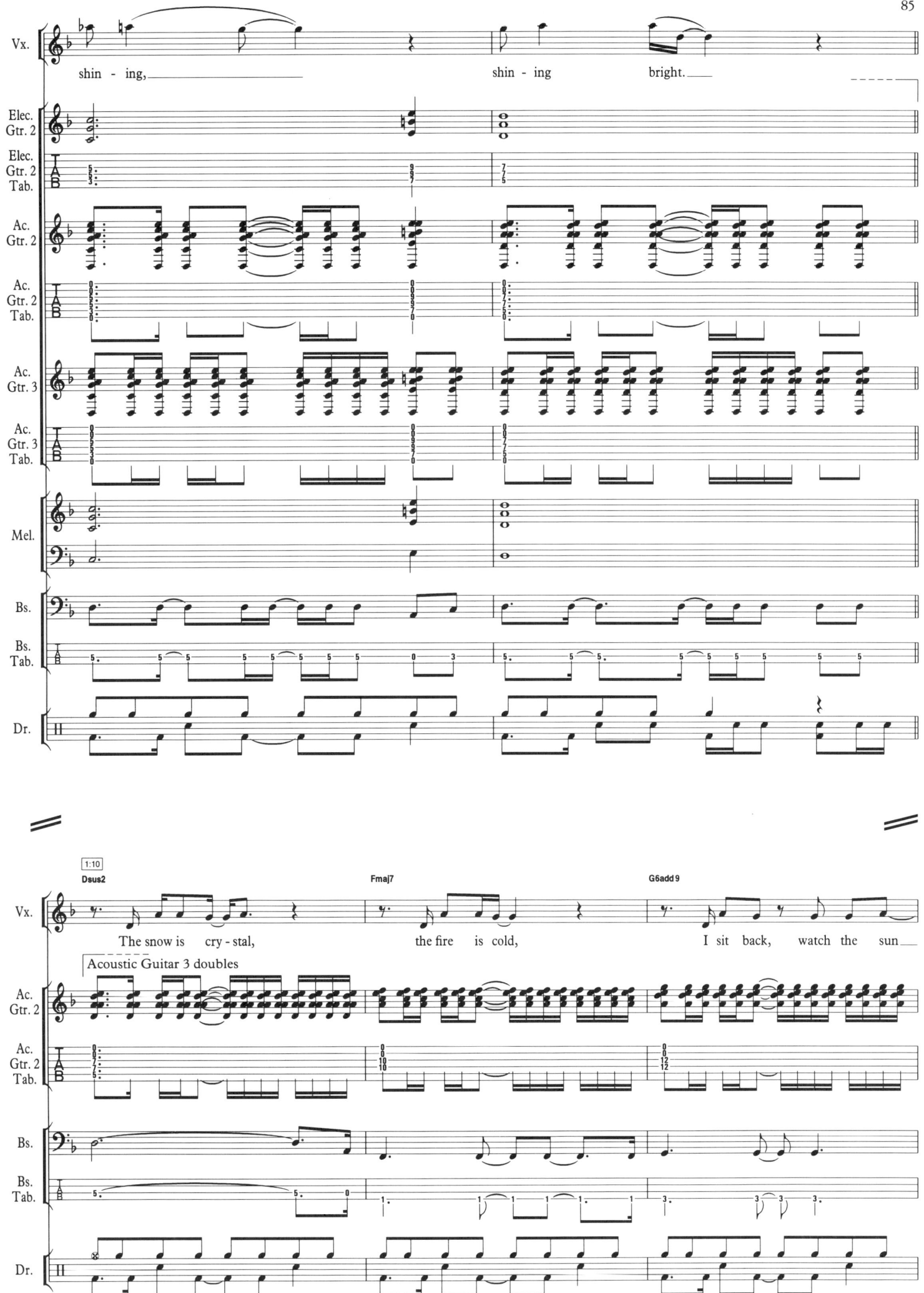

Vx. shin - ing, _____ shin - ing bright. _____

Dsus2   Fmaj7   G6add9

The snow is cry - stal,   the fire is cold,   I sit back, watch the sun _____

Acoustic Guitar 3 doubles

White,   white,   shin - ing,____

Vx.

shin - ing_____ bright - ly.

Elec.
Gtr. 1

Elec.
Gtr. 1
Tab.

7 _____ 7

Elec.
Gtr. 2

Elec.
Gtr. 2
Tab.

7
5

Ac.
Gtr. 2

Acoustic Guitar 3 doubles

Ac.
Gtr. 2
Tab.

Ac.
Gtr. 3

Ac.
Gtr. 3
Tab.

Mel.

Bs.

Bs.
Tab.

5 ____ 5 5 5 5 5 0 ____ 5 ____ 5 ____ 5 ____ 3

Dr.

The hun-ter sits___ on a pure white stal - lion, a hawk in flight, the

bow in his hand. A deer ap-proach-es at the edge___ of the fo-rest,

the ar-row flies, blood on the snow. I said ma-ma said

white, yeah white, shin - ing,

Electric Guitar 3 doubles

Vx.

shin-ing bright - ly. White, white,

Elec.
Gtr. 1

Elec.
Gtr. 1
Tab.

Elec.
Gtr. 2

Elec.
Gtr. 2
Tab.

Ac.
Gtr. 2

Ac.
Gtr. 2
Tab.

Ac.
Gtr. 3

Ac.
Gtr. 3
Tab.

Mel.

Bs.

Bs.
Tab.

Dr.

white,_____ white, shin - ing.

96

Snow is cry - stal,_____

Acoustic Guitar 3 doubles

sun turn to gold. __

Vx.

Earth in the morn-ing said white,_____

Elec.
Gtr. 1

feedback

Elec.
Gtr. 1
Tab.

Elec.
Gtr. 3

feedback
8va

Elec.
Gtr. 3
Tab.

Ac.
Gtr. 2

Ac.
Gtr. 2
Tab.

Ac.
Gtr. 3

Ac.
Gtr. 3
Tab.

Vx.

a sure cry - stal clear yeah_ vir-gin__ white.

Elec.
Gtr. 1

8va

Elec.
Gtr. 1
Tab.

Elec.
Gtr. 3

Elec.
Gtr. 3
Tab.

Ac.
Gtr. 2

Ac.
Gtr. 2
Tab.

Ac.
Gtr. 3

Ac.
Gtr. 3
Tab.

lost to us,   wil-der-ness we reach out,   wil-der-ness we must em-brace you

feel it,   ooh

(spoken) When the barbarians approach
on the frontiers of a civili -

- zation it is a sign of a crisis in that   civilization. When the barbarians come,   not with weapons of war but songs and icons of

Vx.

peace, it is a sign that the crisis is one of a spiritual nature, that's a spiritual nature. We have forgotten our spiritual nature 'cause we're

Elec.
Gtr. 1

Elec.
Gtr. 1
Tab.

Elec.
Gtr. 2

Elec.
Gtr. 2
Tab.

Ac.
Gtr. 2

Ac.
Gtr. 2
Tab.

Mel.

Bs.

Bs.
Tab.

Dr.

wrapped up in too much shit all day, all night.   Can you give me__   white,_____

110

Kiss the earth I said ma-ma said   white. ___

114

116

White,____

white,

118

rit.

Vx. shin - ing,_____ shin - ing bright,_____ yeah._____

(8va)_____ *feedback*

a tempo (♩ = 73)

6:00

Vx. Shin - ing, shin-ing bright - ly, earth mo-ther,

Bass detuned for end section

120

Vx.: white.   Ci-ty drag-gin' me down,___   that's grey,

Vx.: life ___   is grey.___   Got to

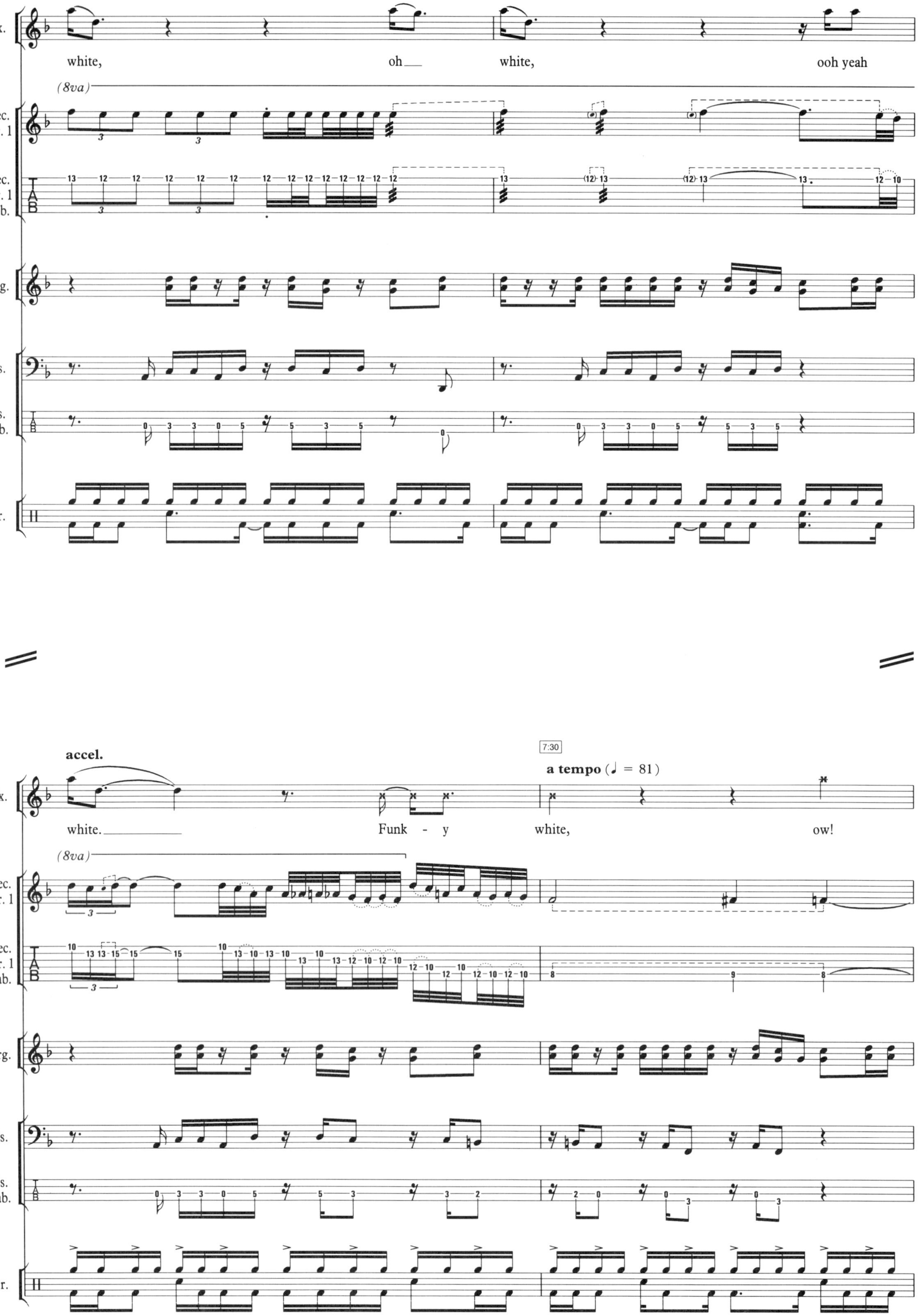
Vx.
white,
oh
white,
ooh yeah
(8va)
Elec. Gtr. 1
Elec. Gtr. 1 Tab.
Org.
Bs.
Bs. Tab.
Dr.
accel.
7:30
a tempo (♩ = 81)
white.
Funk - y
white,
ow!

If

Words & Music by
Ian Astbury and Billy Duffy

0:50
A5
Cadd9
D
A5
Vx.
— yeah.
If the winds of change ___
would blow in the fa-vour of man, ___
re -
Guitar 3 doubles
Gtr. 2
Gtr. 2 Tab.
Pno.
Bs.
Bs. Tab.
Dr.

Cadd9
G5
[A]
Vx.
- solve this ___ si - tu - a - tion, ___
un - do the work of i - dle temp - ta - tion.
Gtr. 2
Gtr. 2 Tab.
Gtr. 3
Gtr. 3 Tab.
Bs.
Bs. Tab.
Dr.

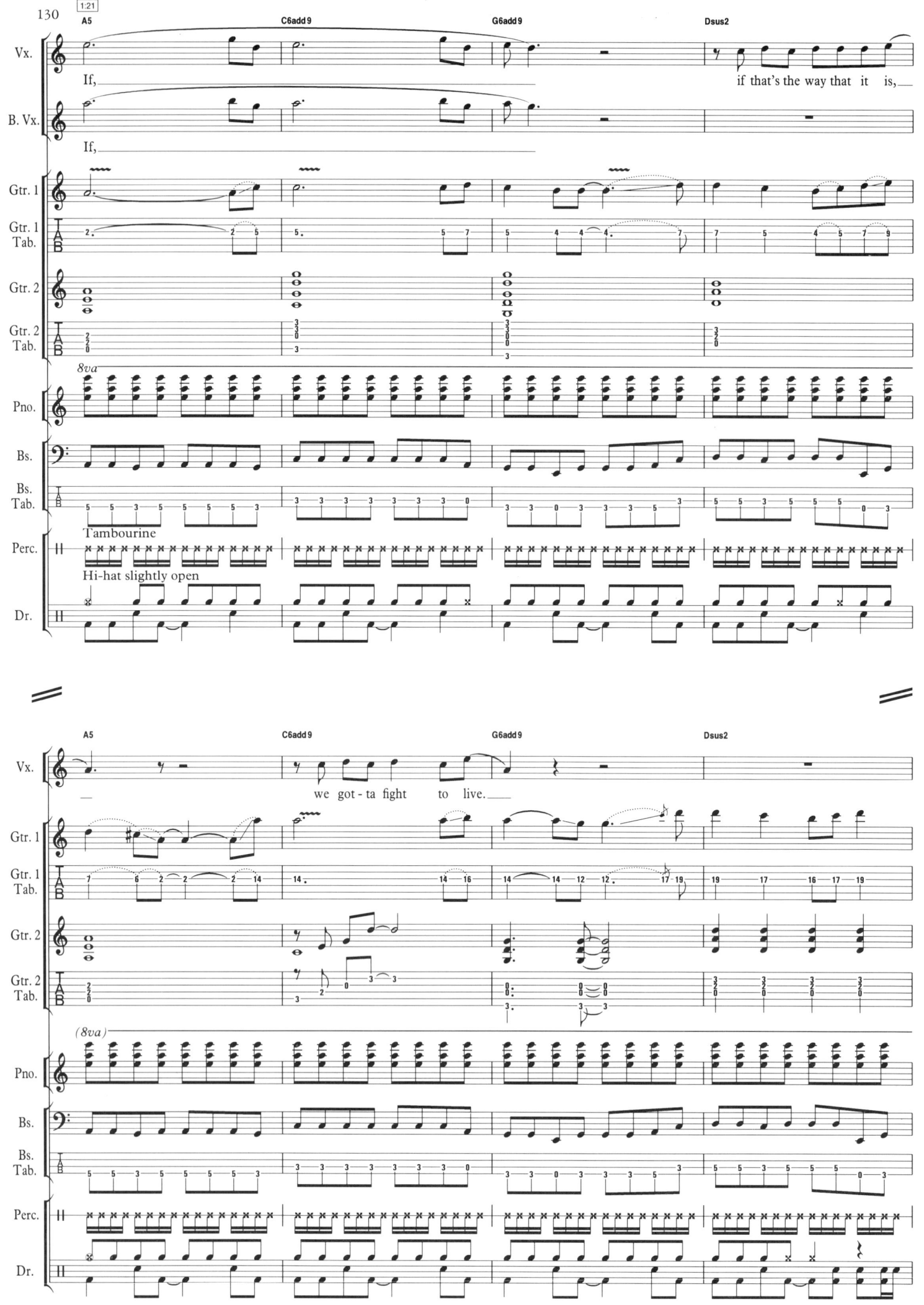

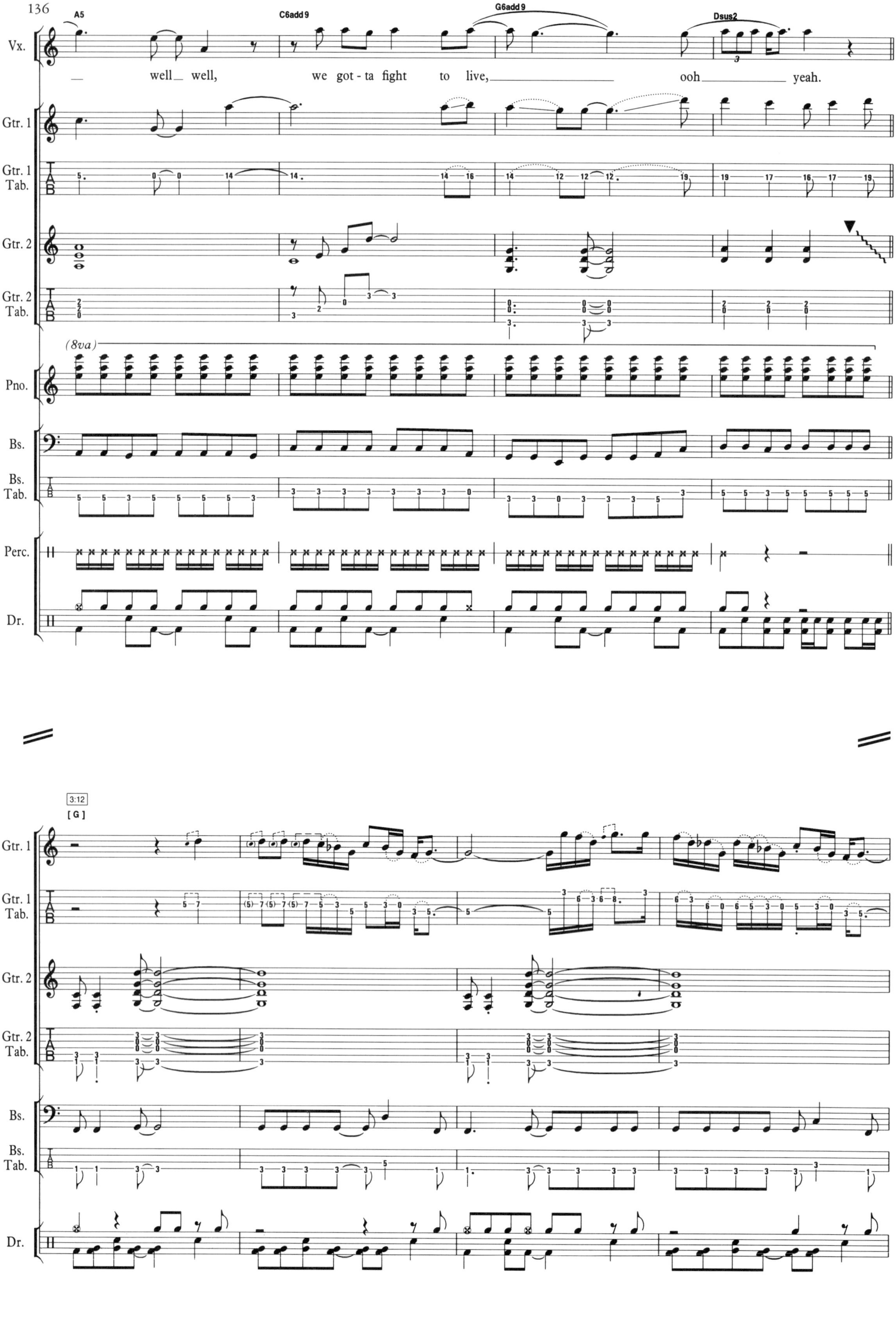
A5
C6add9
G6add9
Dsus2
Vx.
— well_ well, we got-ta fight to live,_______ ooh_______ yeah.
Gtr. 1
Gtr. 1 Tab.
Gtr. 2
Gtr. 2 Tab.
(8va)
Pno.
Bs.
Bs. Tab.
Perc.
Dr.
3:12
[G]
Gtr. 1
Gtr. 1 Tab.
Gtr. 2
Gtr. 2 Tab.
Bs.
Bs. Tab.
Dr.

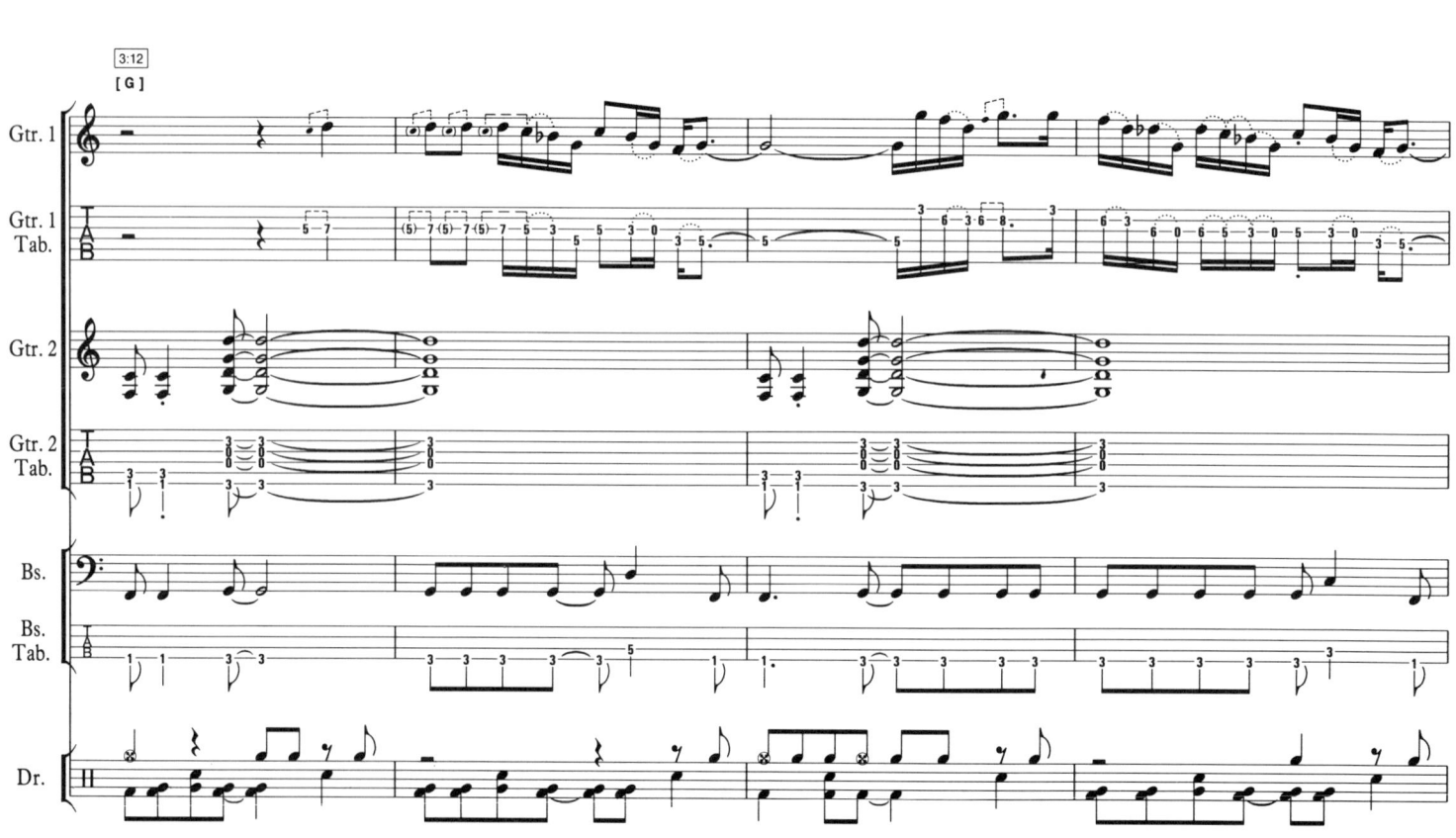

Run - nin' out of time now,_____ come_____

Gadd9
D5
A5
Vx.
ow!
ooh yeah yeah yeah yeah.
8va
Gtr. 1
Gtr. 1 Tab.
Gtr. 2
Gtr. 2 Tab.
Pno.
Bs.
Bs. Tab.
Perc.
Dr.
C6add9
G6add9
(8va)

144

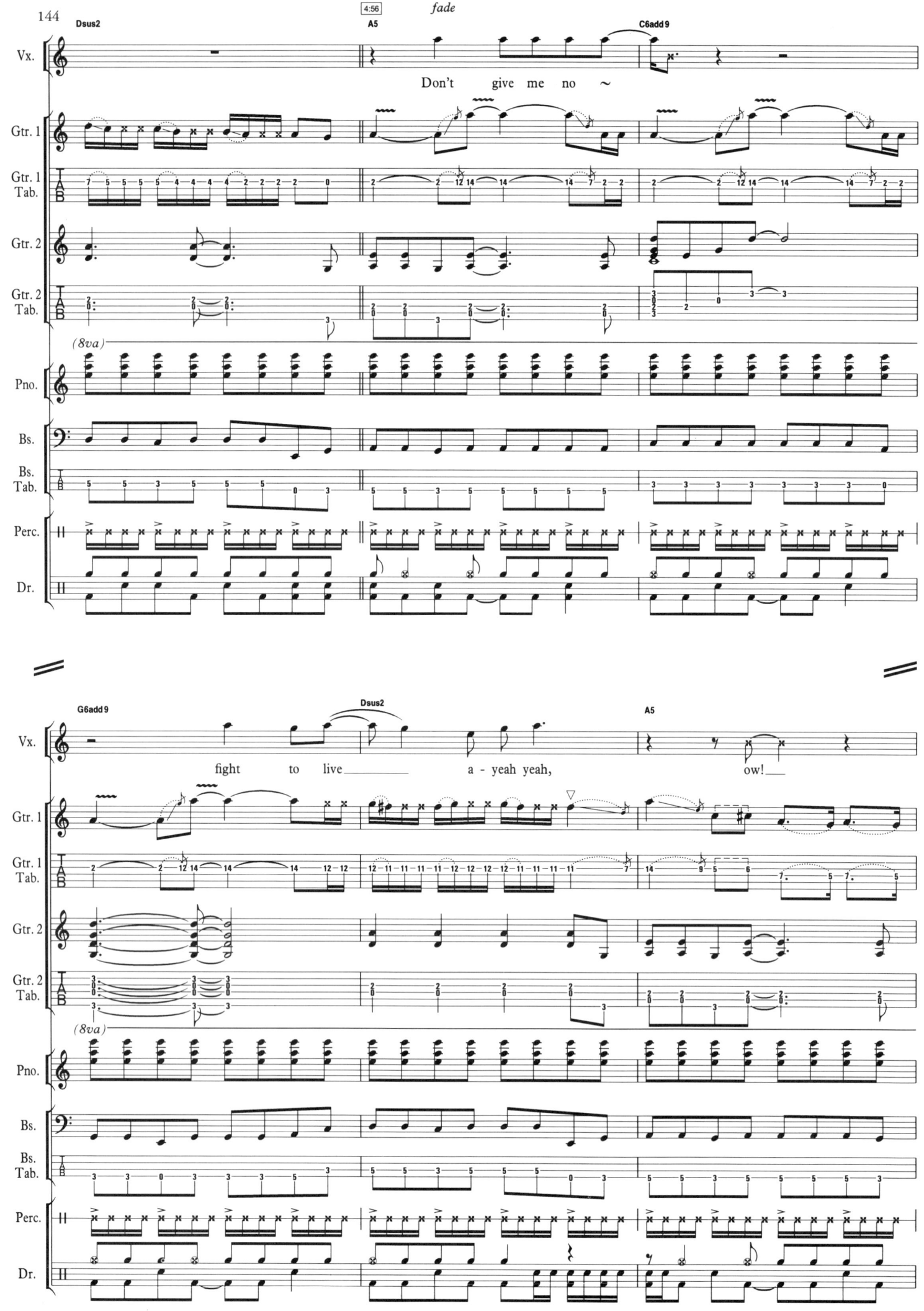

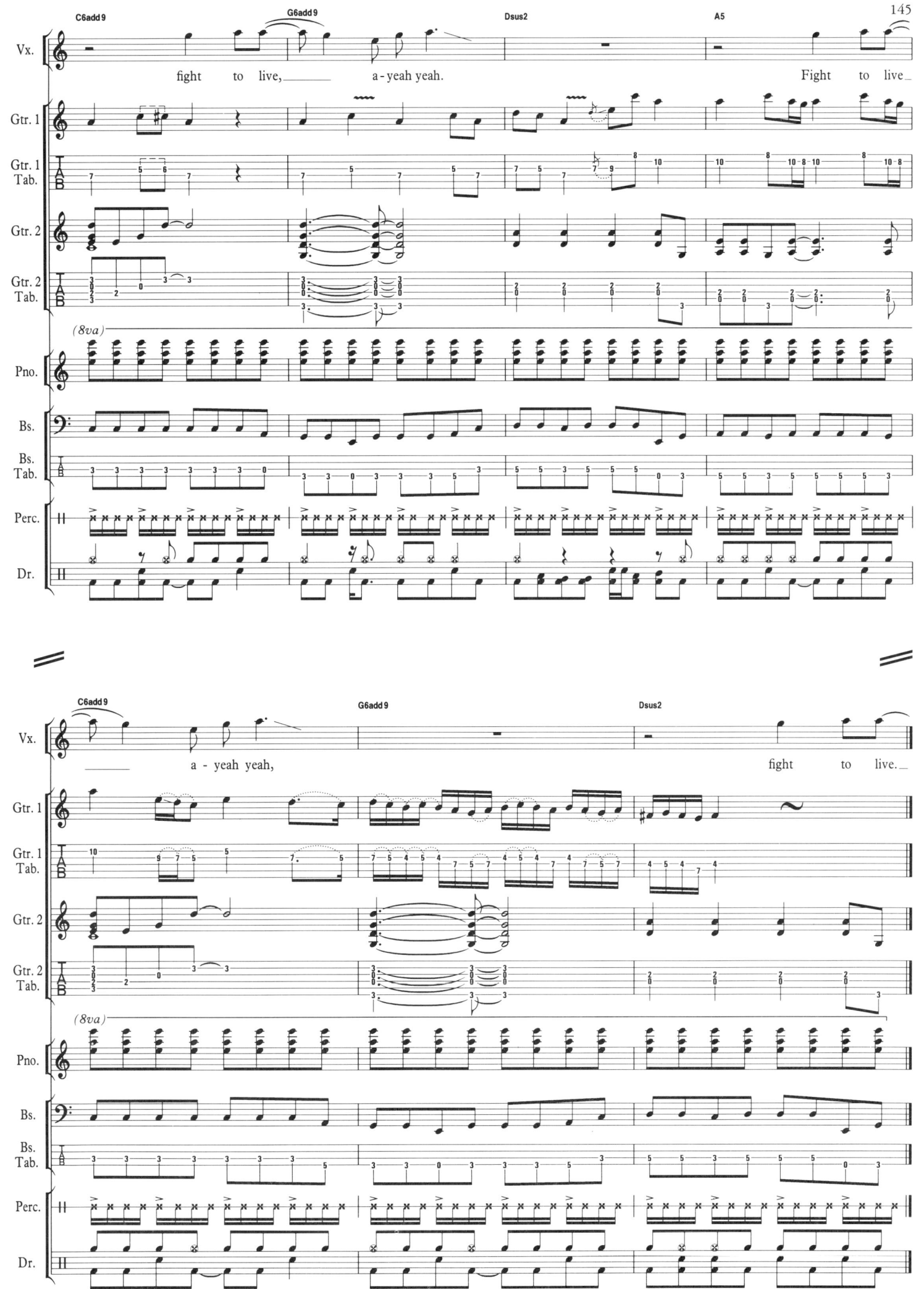

Full Tilt

Words & Music by
Ian Astbury and Billy Duffy

152

154

Su-per fat funk - y.

3:03

wah-wah   Wow!

[E]
Vx.
a - liv - in', do it.
Gtr. 3
Gtr. 3 Tab.
Bs.
Bs. Tab.
Dr.
3:36
[E] D A D [E] D A D
8va
Gtr. 1
Gtr. 1 Tab.
Gtr. 3
Gtr. 3 Tab.
Bs.
Bs. Tab.
Dr.

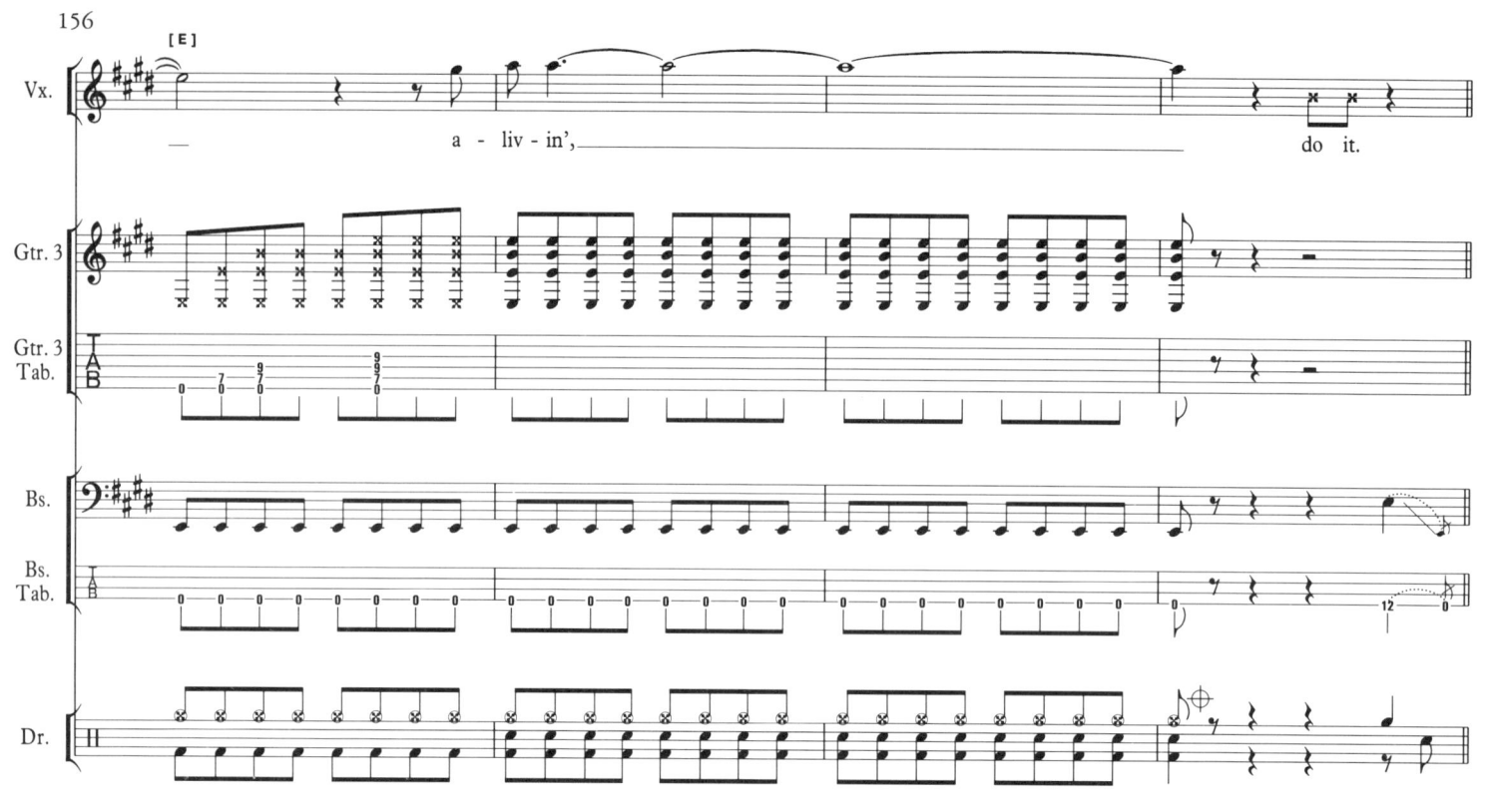

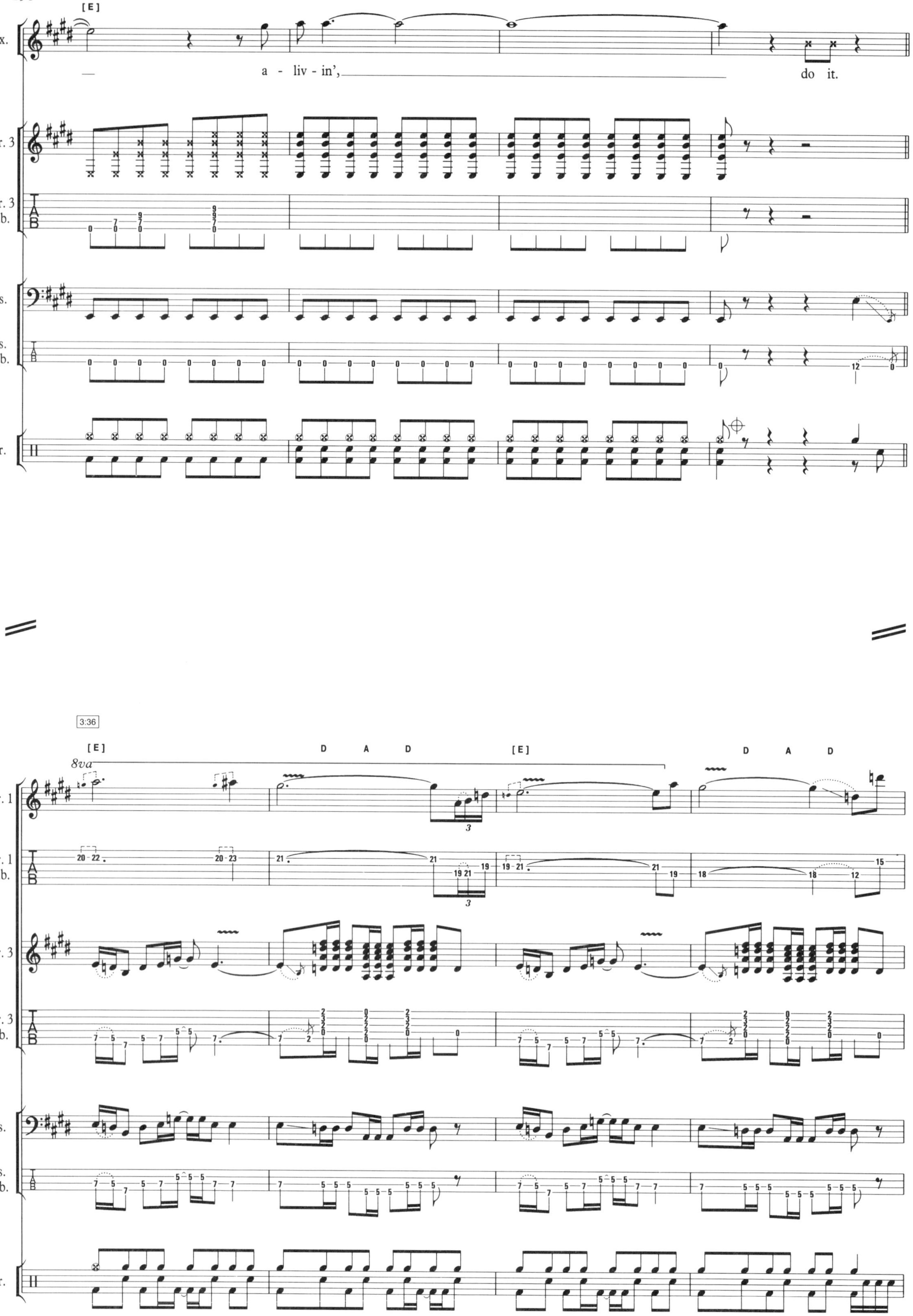

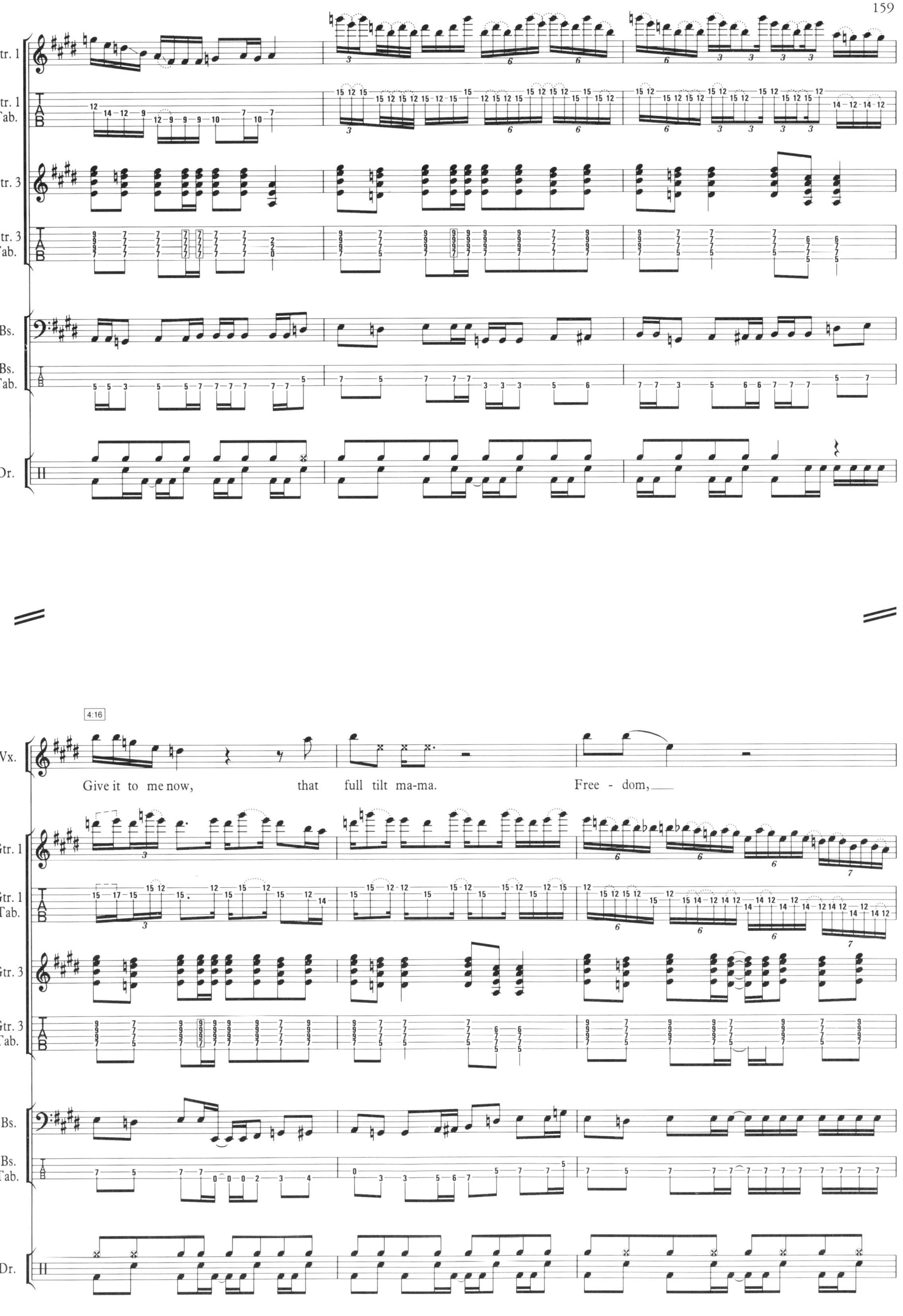

Give it to me now, that full tilt ma-ma. Free - dom,

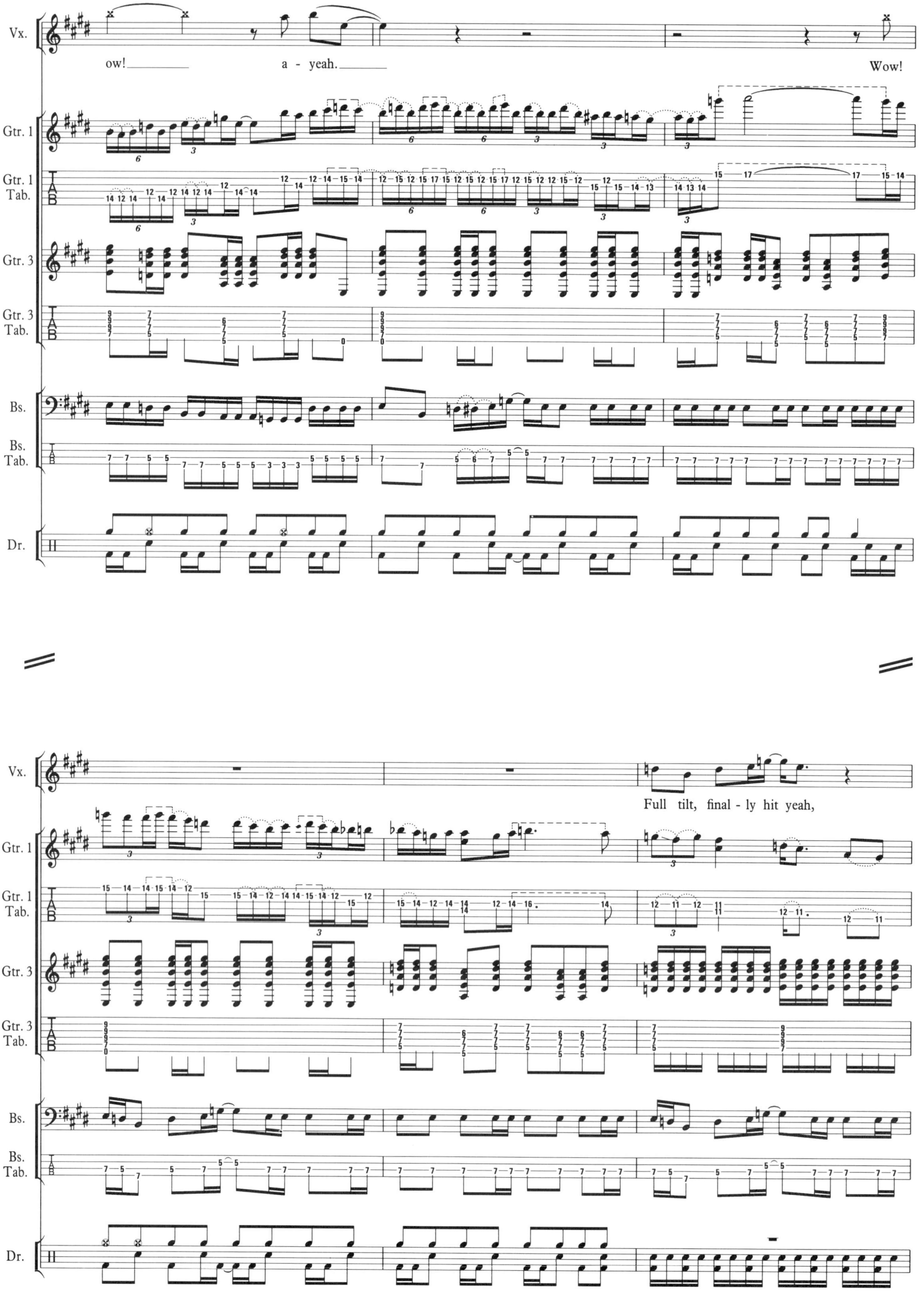
Vx.
ow! a - yeah. Wow!
Gtr. 1
Gtr. 1 Tab.
Gtr. 3
Gtr. 3 Tab.
Bs.
Bs. Tab.
Dr.
Full tilt, final - ly hit yeah,

Heart of Soul

Words & Music by
Ian Astbury and Billy Duffy

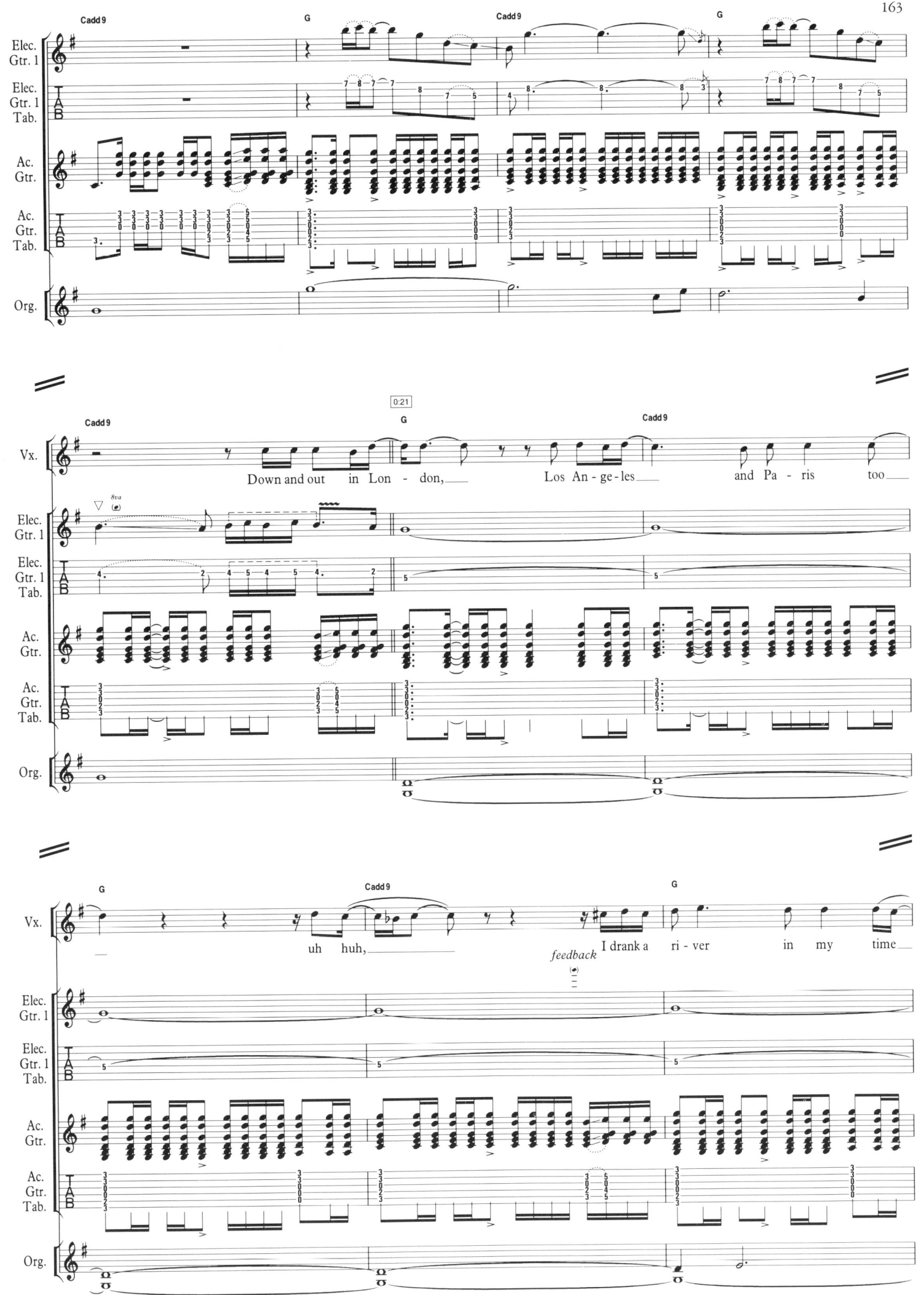

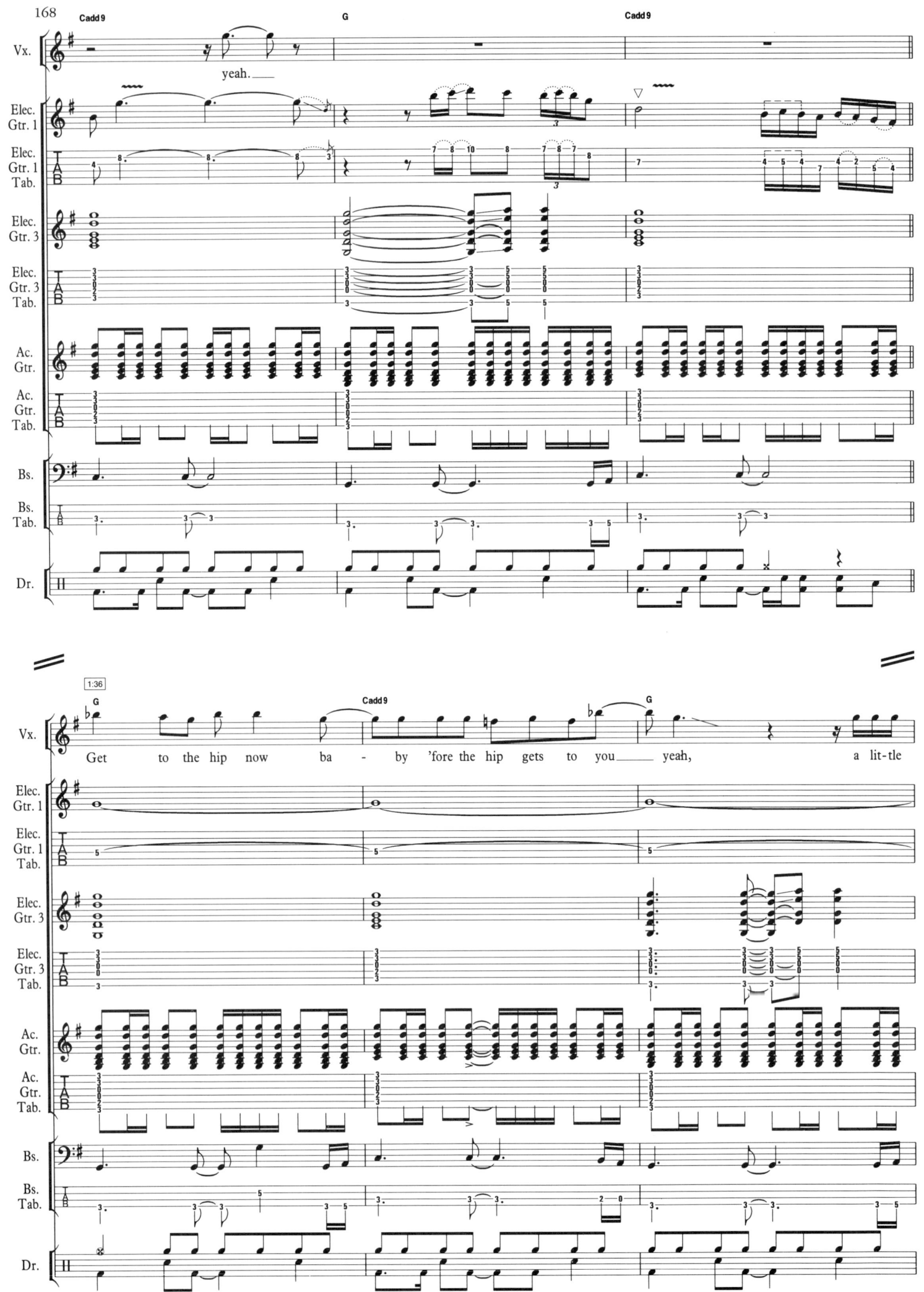

Get to the hip now baby 'fore the hip gets to you_____ yeah, a lit-tle

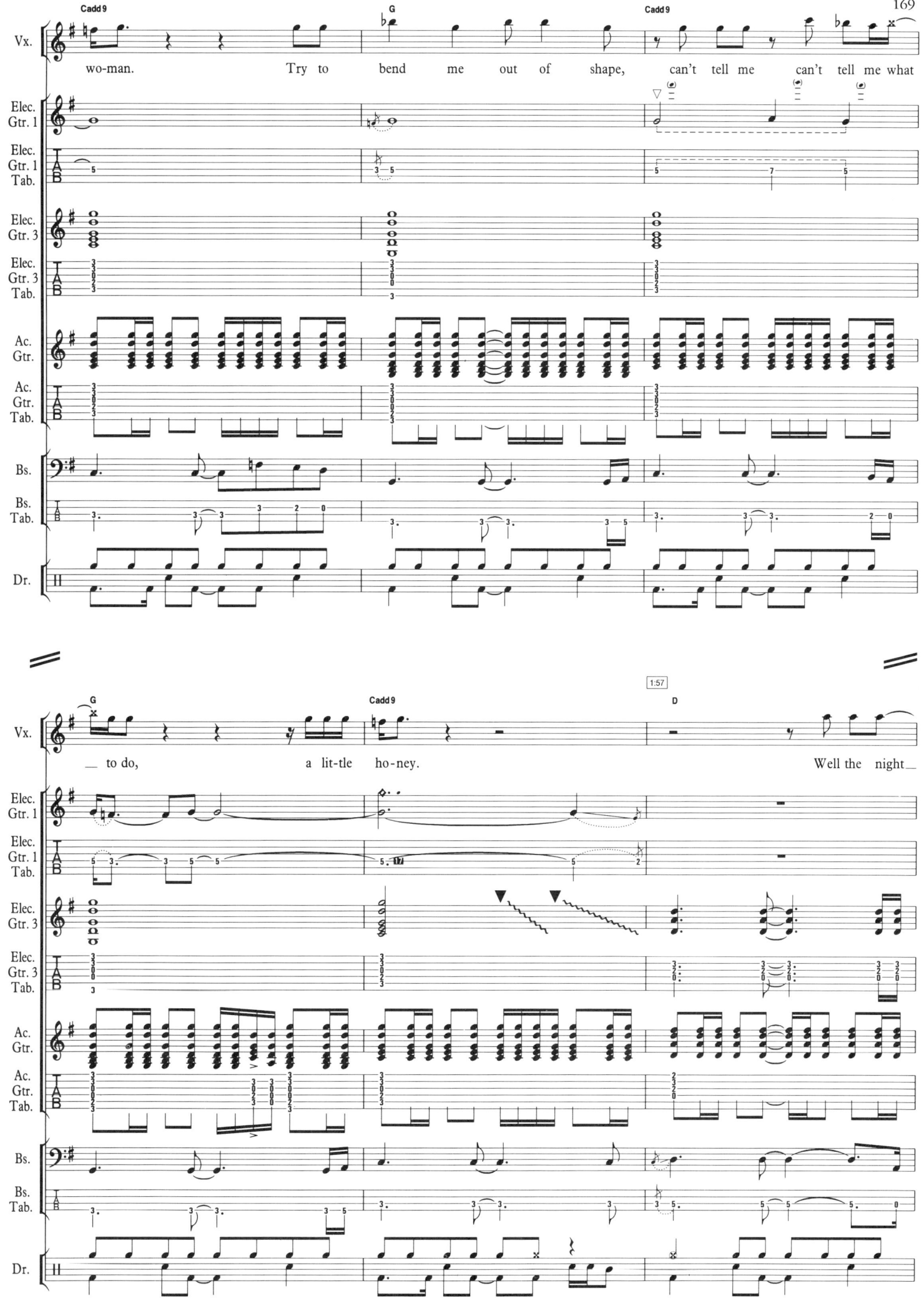

172

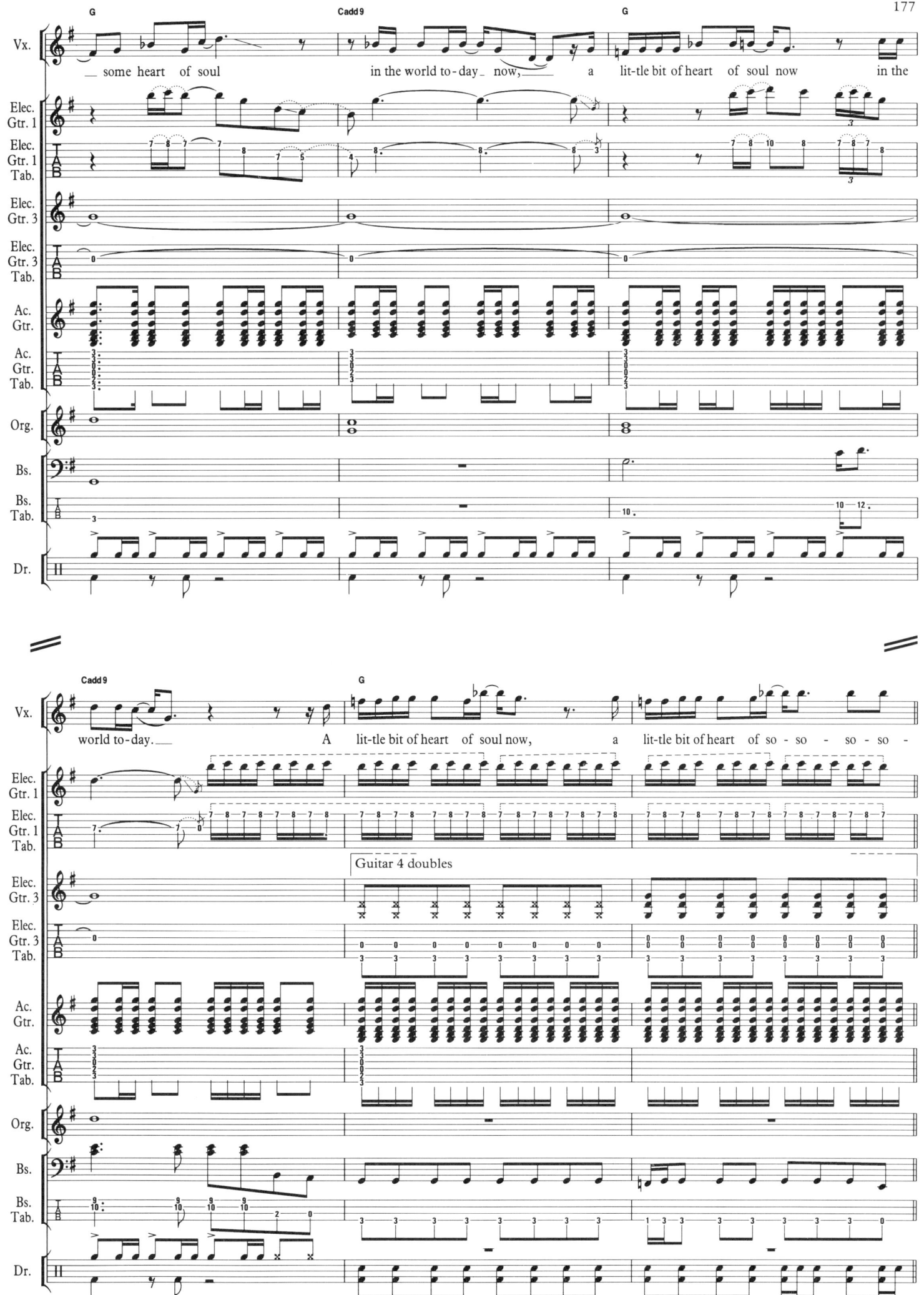

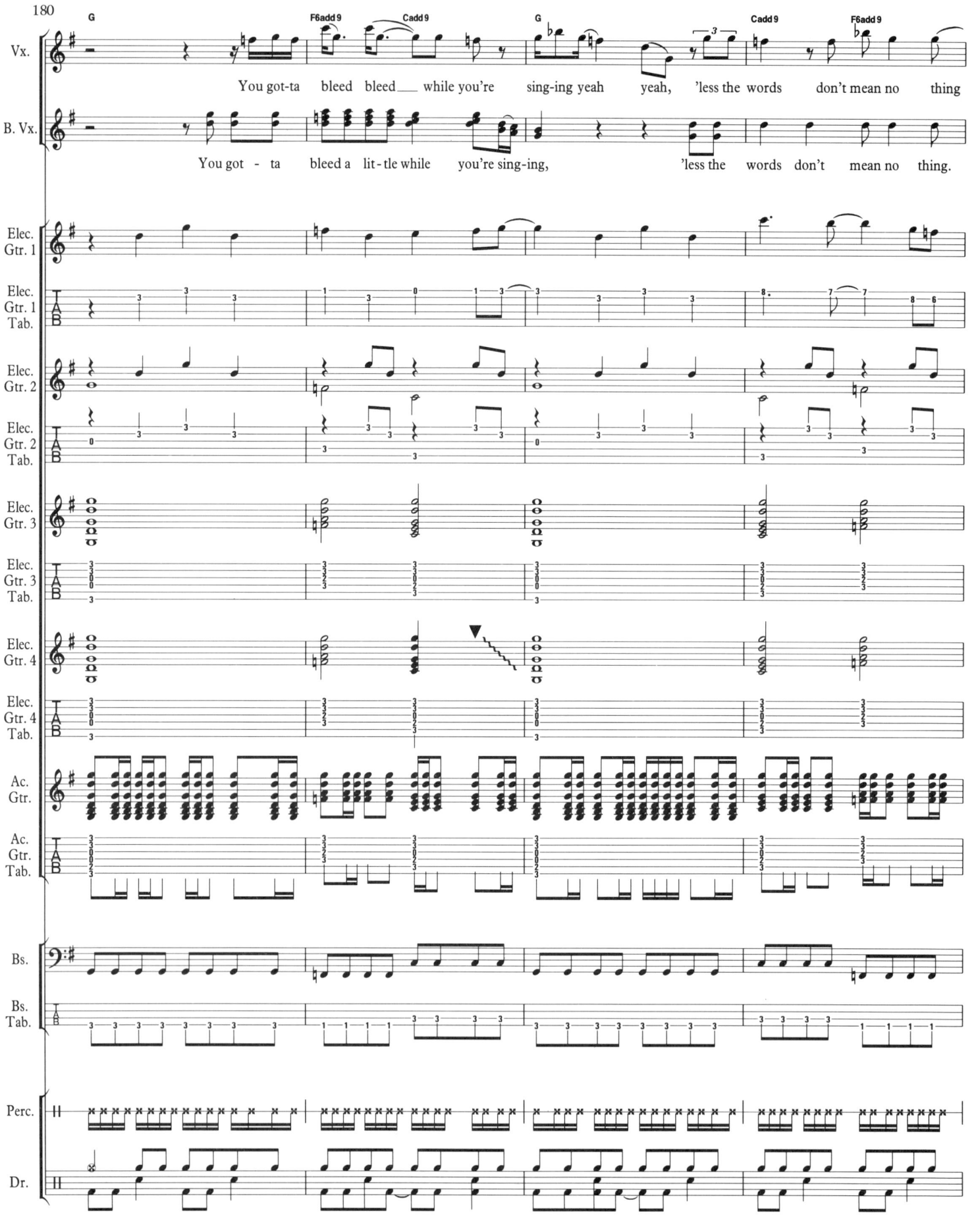

184

what   I want, what I want, what I want   is__ a heart of soul,   what   I want, what I want, what I need now

you got   the heart   of soul_ yeah.   You got   the pow - er,   you got   the soul,

you got the heart of soul yeah.   You got the pow-er,   we got the heart,   we got the heart of   soul.

Bangkok Rain

Words & Music by
Ian Astbury and Billy Duffy

Black___ night ba - by,___

196

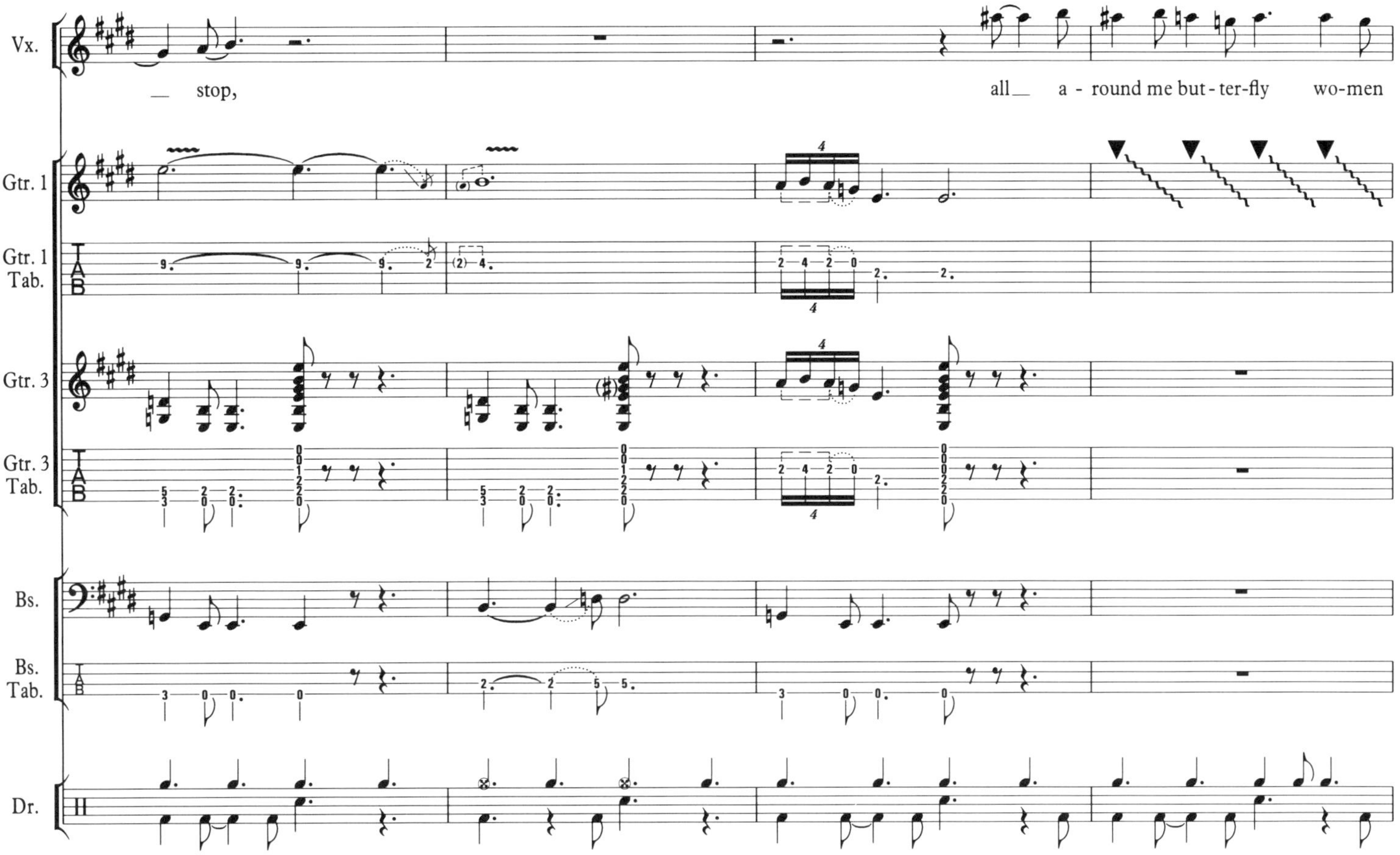
Vx.
— stop,
all — a - round me but - ter-fly wo-men
Gtr. 1
Gtr. 1 Tab.
Gtr. 3
Gtr. 3 Tab.
Bs.
Bs. Tab.
Dr.

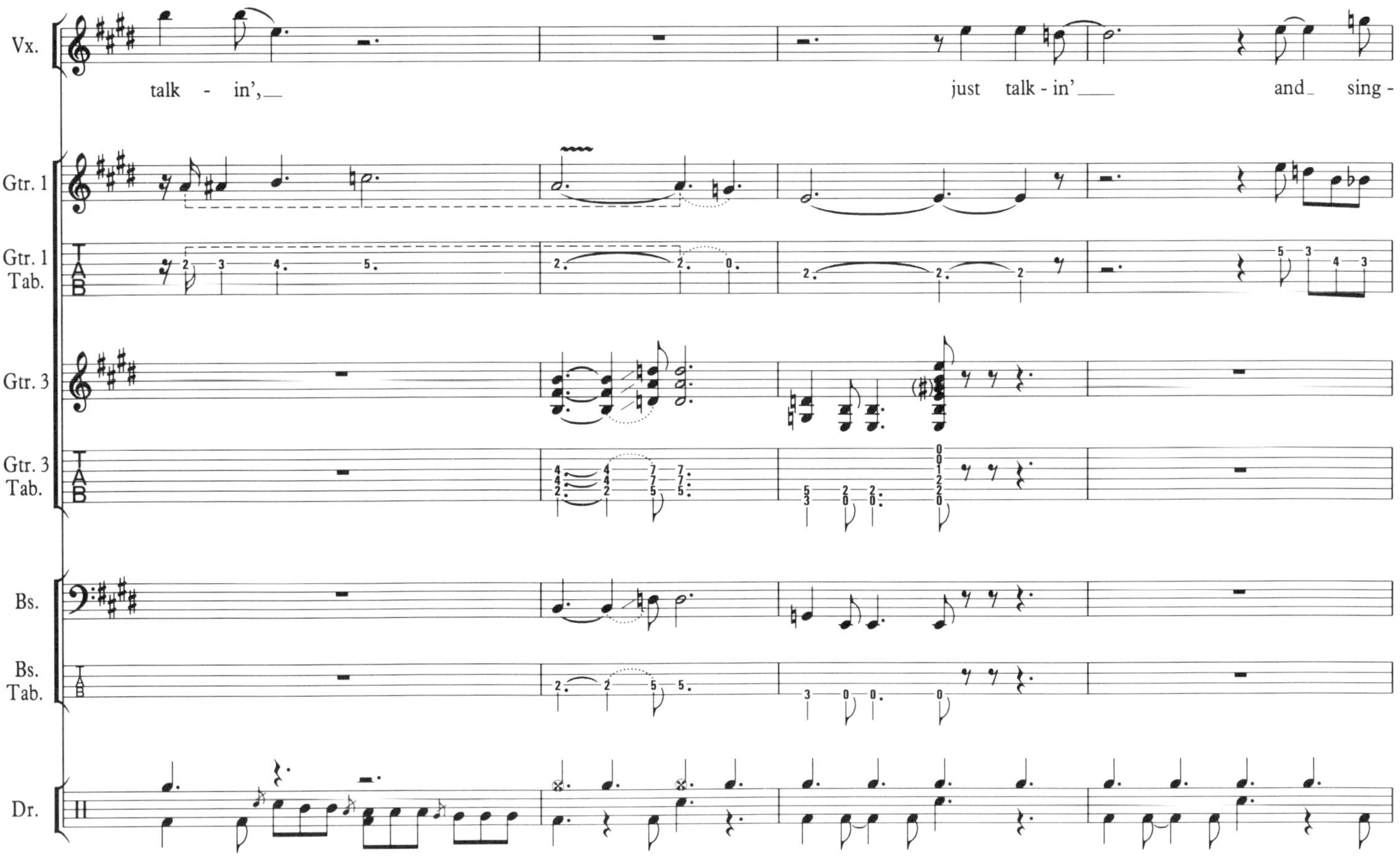
Vx.
talk - in', —
just talk - in' —
and — sing -
Gtr. 1
Gtr. 1 Tab.
Gtr. 3
Gtr. 3 Tab.
Bs.
Bs. Tab.
Dr.

198

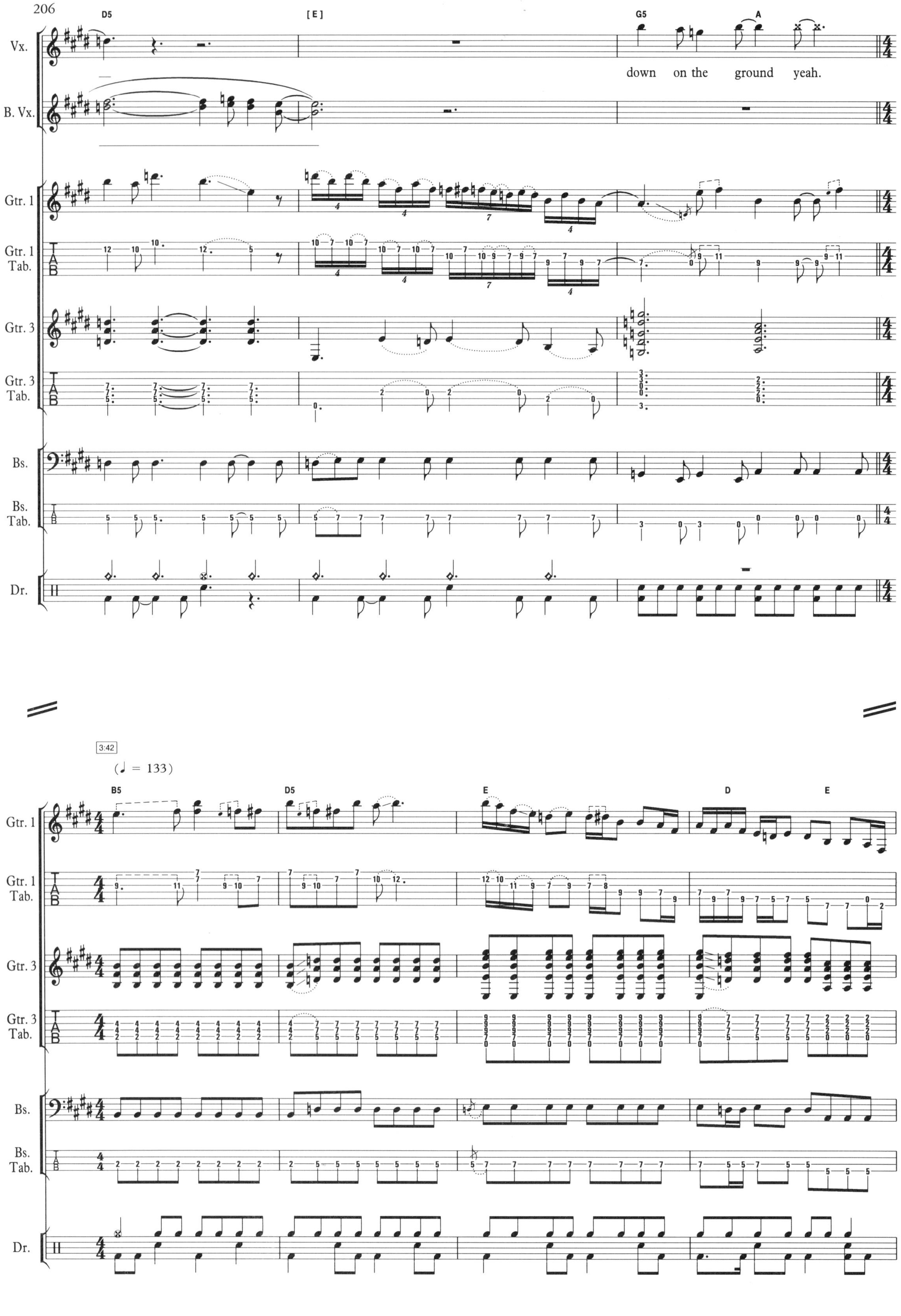
D5
[E]
G5
A
down on the ground yeah.
Vx.
B. Vx.
Gtr. 1
Gtr. 1 Tab.
Gtr. 3
Gtr. 3 Tab.
Bs.
Bs. Tab.
Dr.
3:42
(♩ = 133)
B5
D5
E
D
E

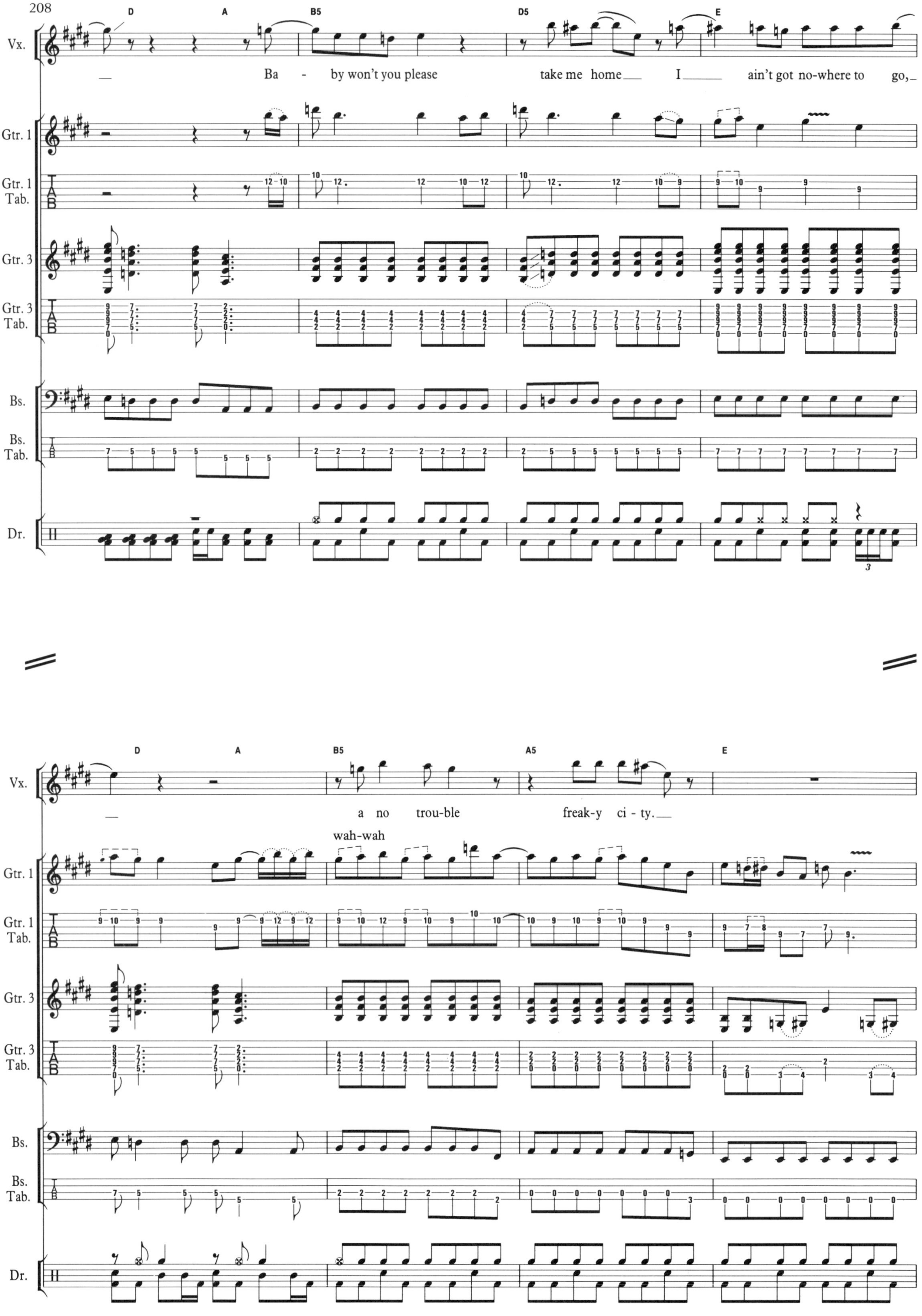
D A B5 D5 E
Vx.
Baby won't you please take me home I ain't got no-where to go,
Gtr. 1
Gtr. 1 Tab.
Gtr. 3
Gtr. 3 Tab.
Bs.
Bs. Tab.
Dr.
D A B5 A5 E
Vx.
a no trou-ble freak-y ci-ty.
wah-wah
Gtr. 1
Gtr. 1 Tab.
Gtr. 3
Gtr. 3 Tab.
Bs.
Bs. Tab.
Dr.

Freak-y ci - ty,___ freak ci - ty,___ freak ci - ty.___

Freak ci - ty,___ freak ci - ty,___ freak-y ci - ty.___

212

Indian

Words & Music by
Ian Astbury and Billy Duffy

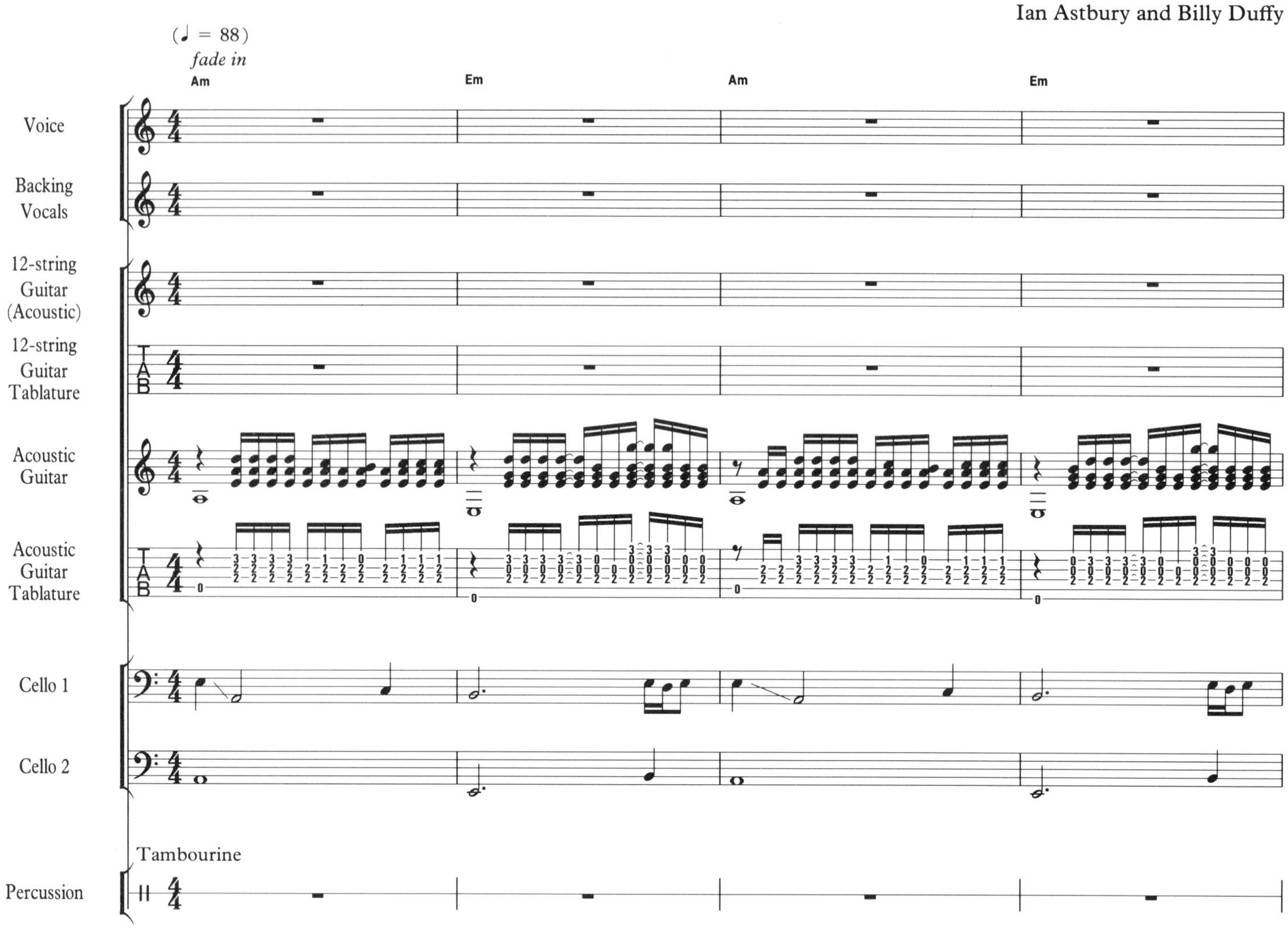

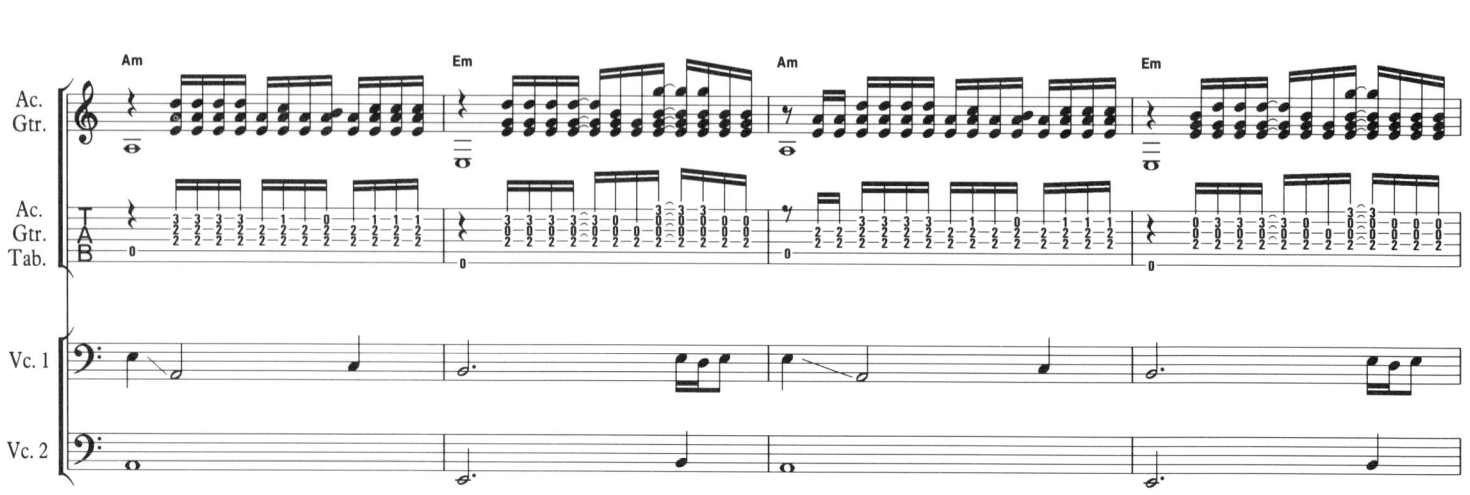

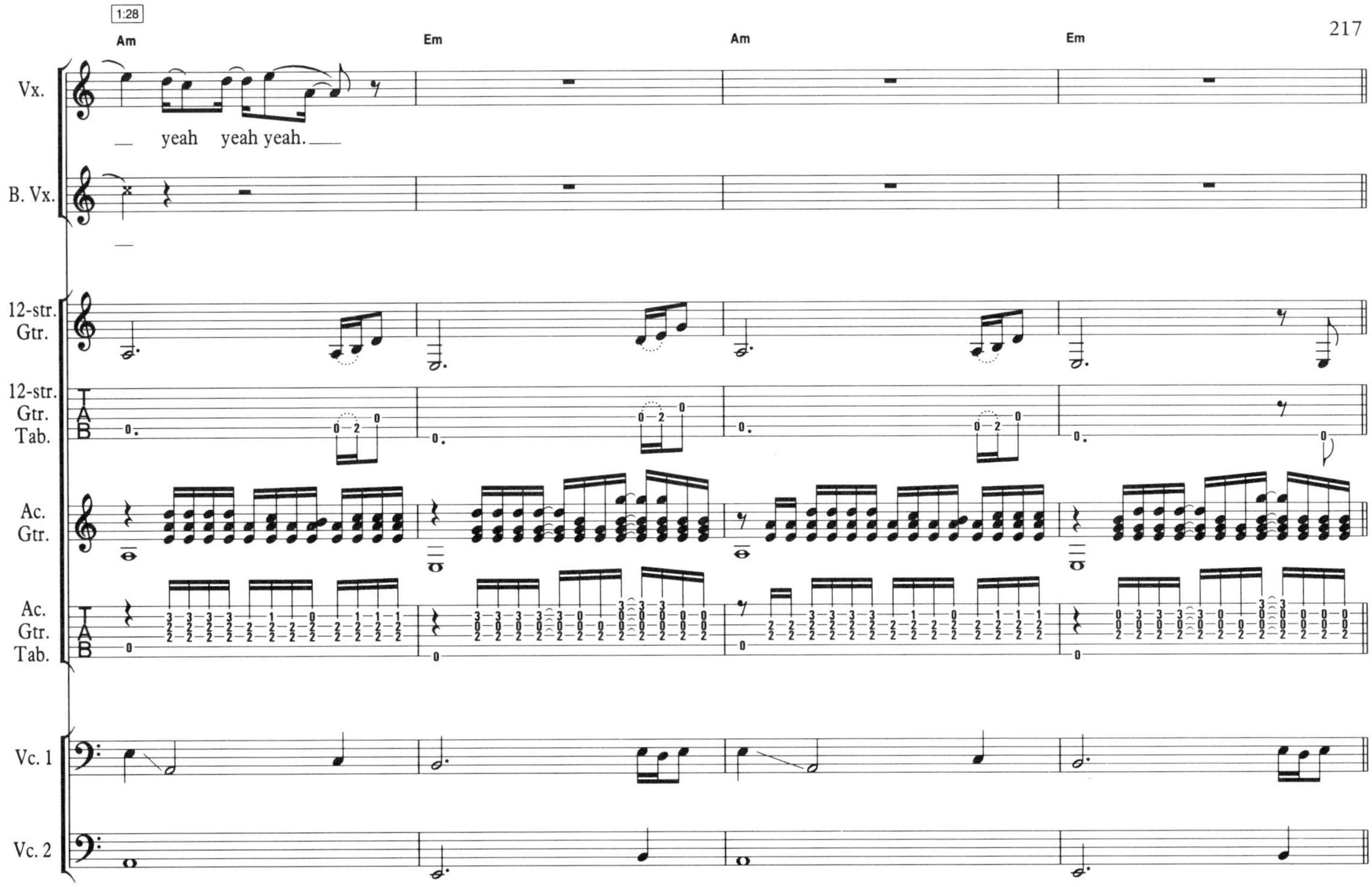
1:28
Am
Em
Am
Em
Vx.
yeah yeah yeah.
B. Vx.
12-str. Gtr.
12-str. Gtr. Tab.
Ac. Gtr.
Ac. Gtr. Tab.
Vc. 1
Vc. 2

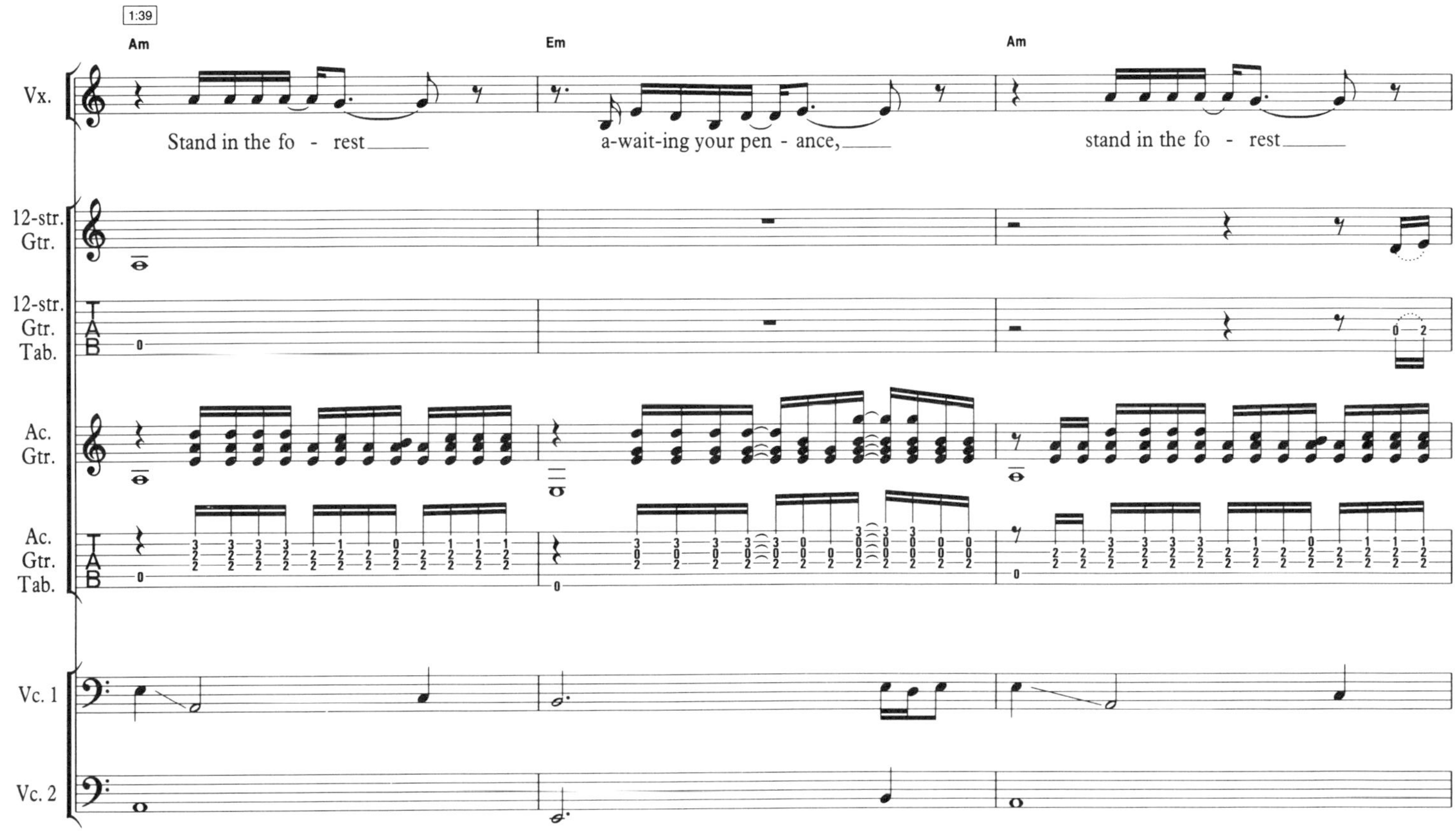
1:39
Am
Em
Am
Vx.
Stand in the fo - rest
a-wait-ing your pen - ance,
stand in the fo - rest
12-str. Gtr.
12-str. Gtr. Tab.
Ac. Gtr.
Ac. Gtr. Tab.
Vc. 1
Vc. 2

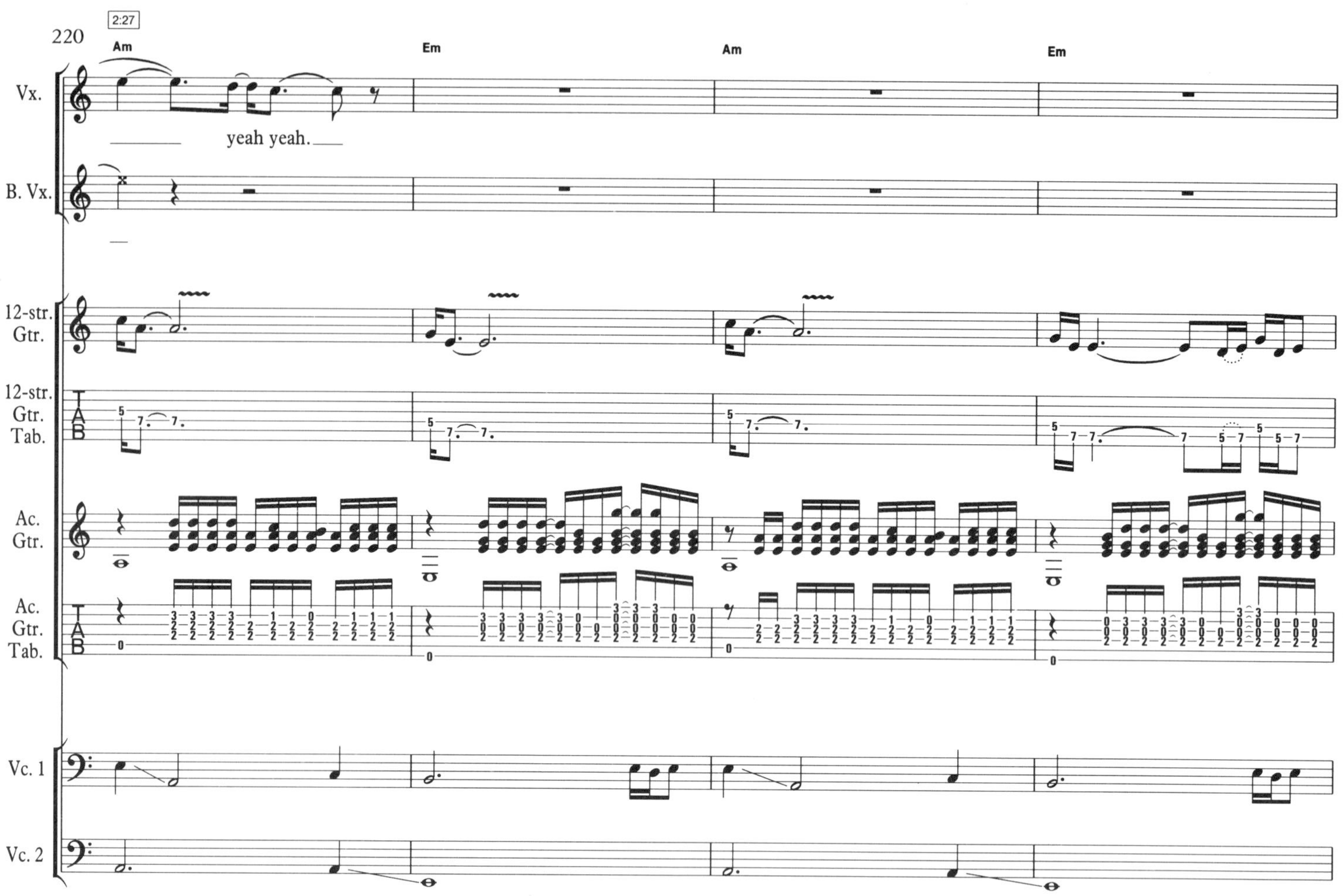
2:27
Am
Em
Am
Em
Vx.
yeah yeah.
B. Vx.
12-str. Gtr.
12-str. Gtr. Tab.
Ac. Gtr.
Ac. Gtr. Tab.
Vc. 1
Vc. 2

Am
Em
Am
Em
12-str. Gtr.
12-str. Gtr. Tab.
Ac. Gtr.
Ac. Gtr. Tab.
Vc. 1
Vc. 2

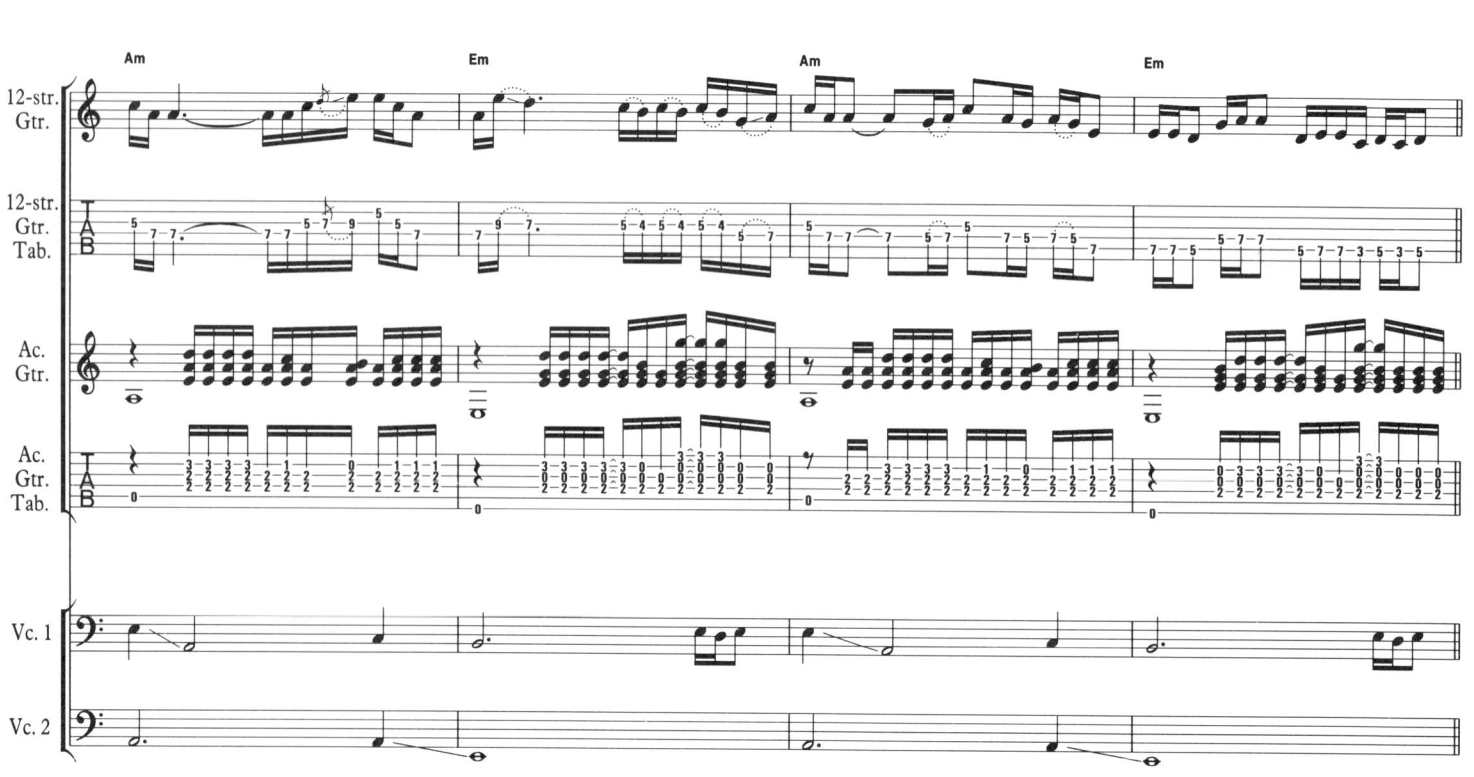

222

Sweet Salvation

Words & Music by
Ian Astbury and Billy Duffy

228

Gadd9
Vx.
no harm — will come be - tween
Ac. Gtr. 2
Ac. Gtr. 2 Tab.
12-str. Gtr.
12-str. Gtr. Tab.
Hmn.
A
D
Vx.
us.
Oh beau - ti - ful,
Ac. Gtr. 2
Ac. Gtr. 2 Tab.
12-str. Gtr.
12-str. Gtr. Tab.
Hmn.

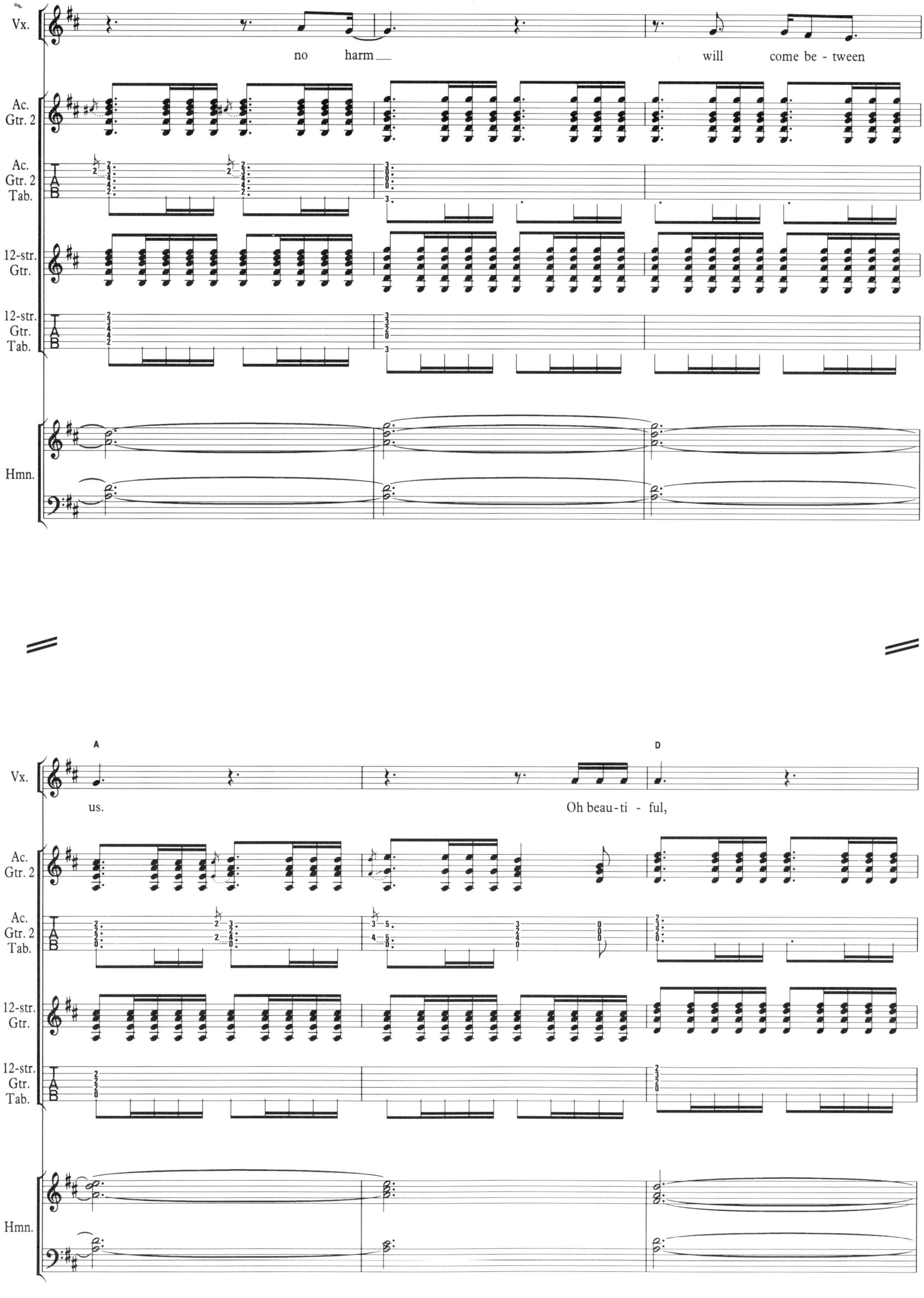

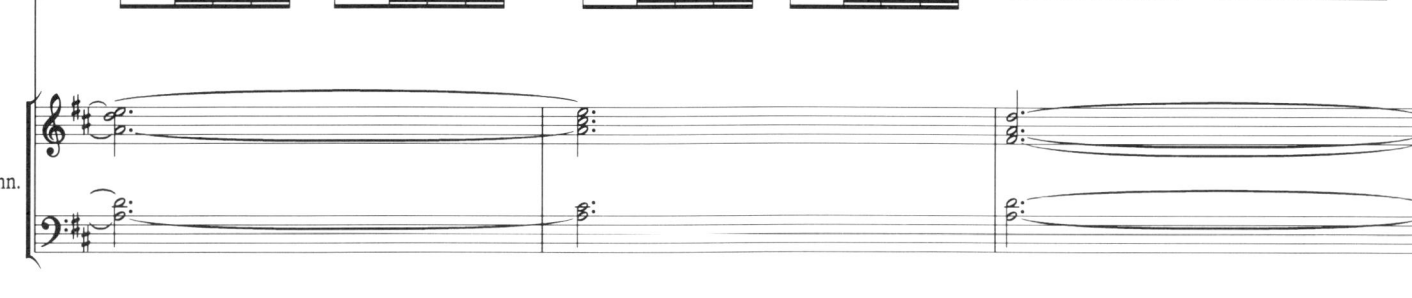

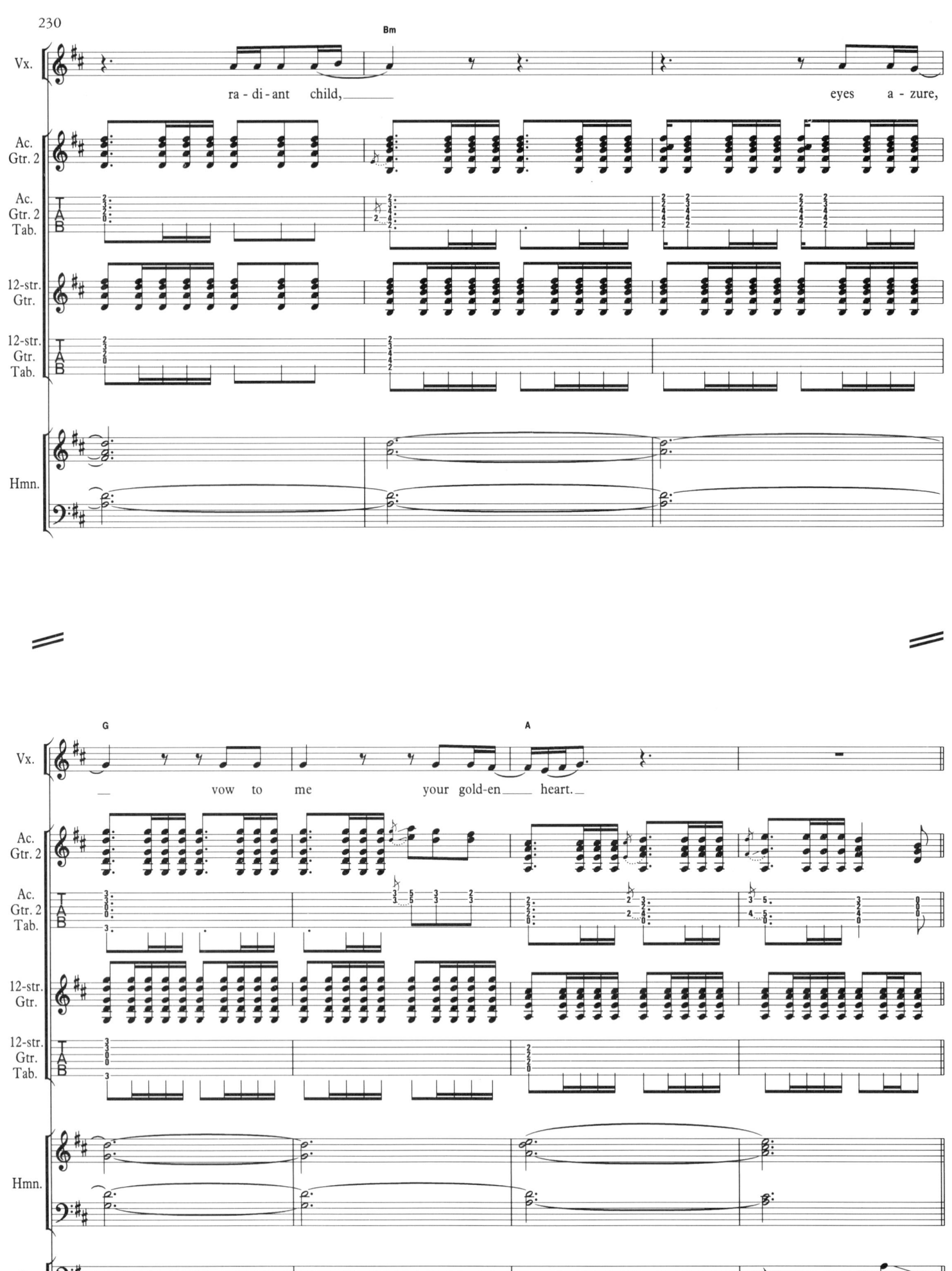

ra - di - ant child,_____ eyes a - zure,

vow to me your gold-en_____ heart.

Se-duced   by   your glance   mm,_____   o - ver-whelmed

236

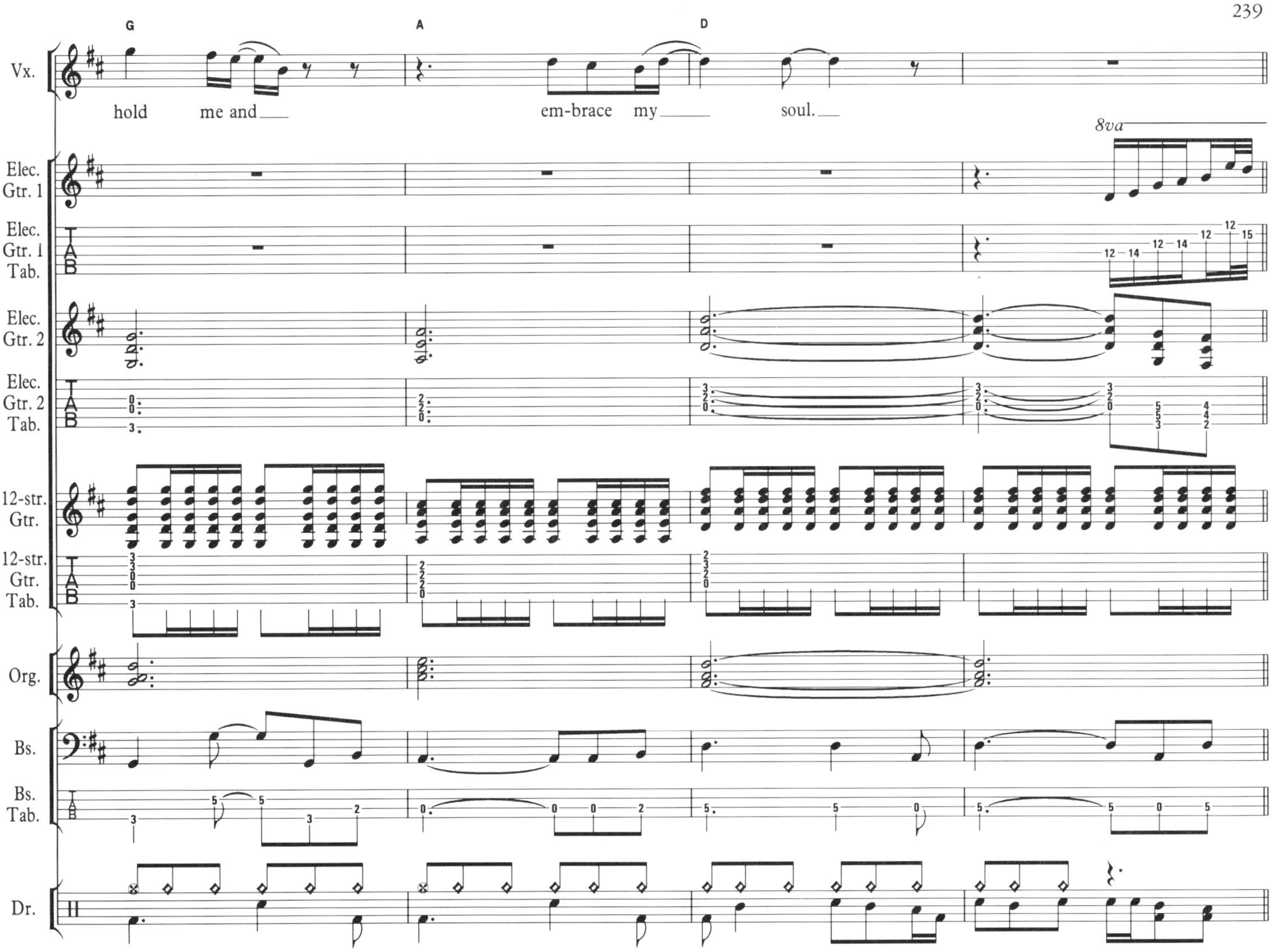
G
A
D
Vx.
hold me and
em-brace my
soul.
8va
Elec. Gtr. 1
Elec. Gtr. 1 Tab.
Elec. Gtr. 2
Elec. Gtr. 2 Tab.
12-str. Gtr.
12-str. Gtr. Tab.
Org.
Bs.
Bs. Tab.
Dr.

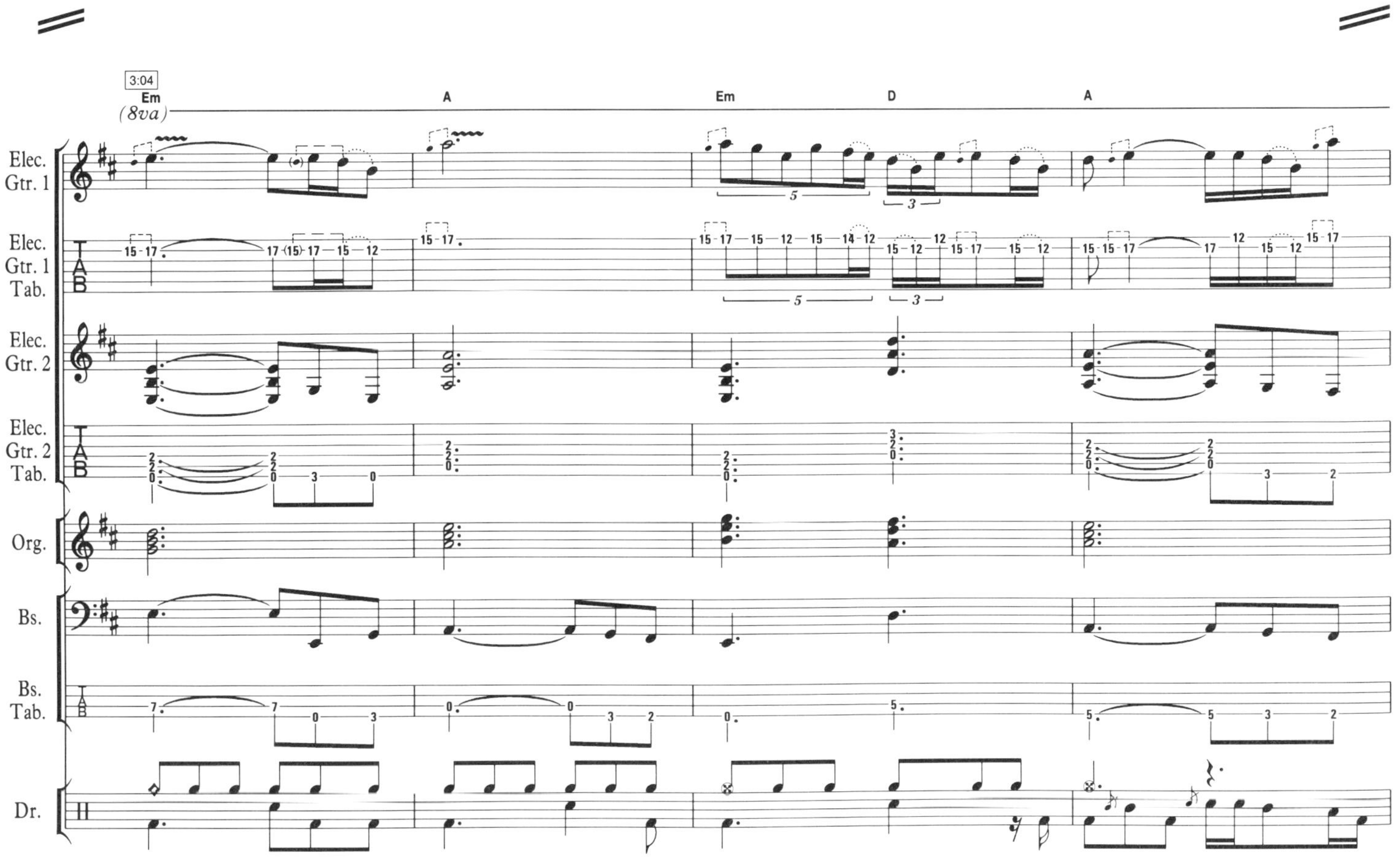
3:04
Em
(8va)
A
Em
D
A
Elec. Gtr. 1
Elec. Gtr. 1 Tab.
Elec. Gtr. 2
Elec. Gtr. 2 Tab.
Org.
Bs.
Bs. Tab.
Dr.

240

- va - tion,

you make me   feel

248

king of the world

wo!

Wonderland

Words & Music by
Ian Astbury and Billy Duffy

succumbing to the he dog sound of a mystifying beat combo that breaks down your door. Gonna take you high now,

take you real high.

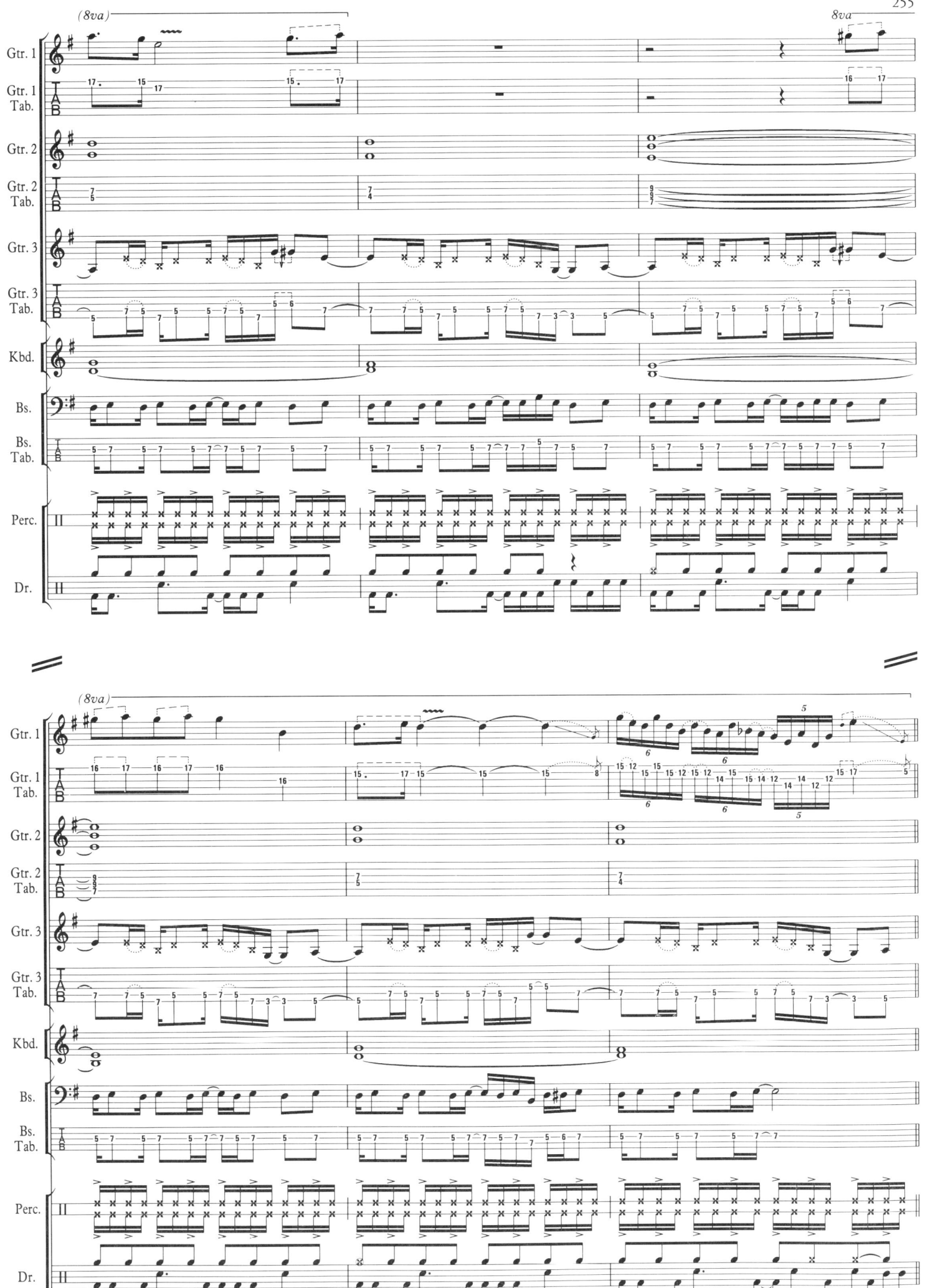

258

-feat - ed__ yeah,___ but not for long,__ no.

Won - der - land,_____

Won - der - land,_____

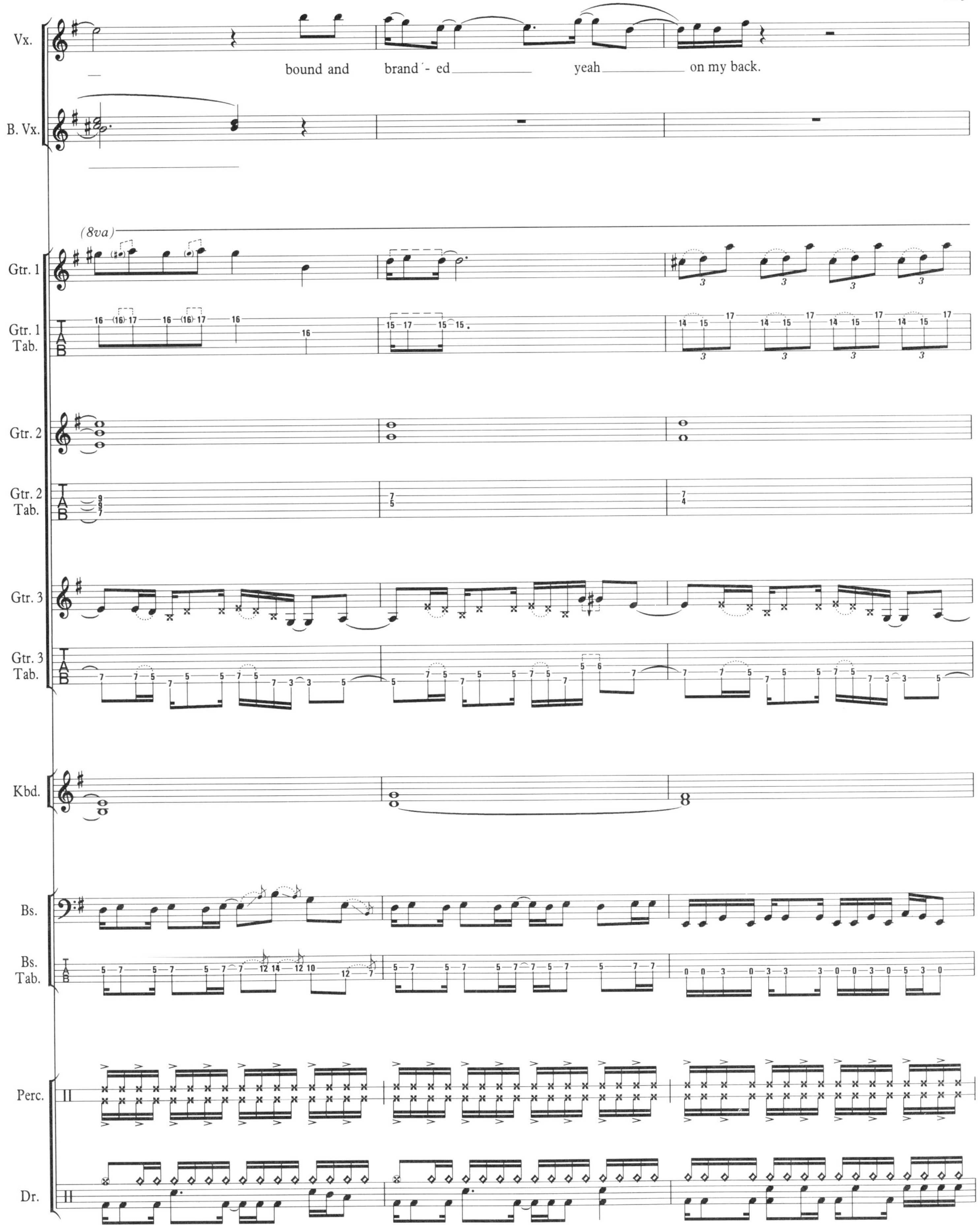
Vx.
bound and brand´- ed yeah on my back.
B. Vx.
(8va)
Gtr. 1
Gtr. 1 Tab.
Gtr. 2
Gtr. 2 Tab.
Gtr. 3
Gtr. 3 Tab.
Kbd.
Bs.
Bs. Tab.
Perc.
Dr.

ooh yeah yeah yeah yeah.

sound of a mystifying beat combo that's gonna take you ...high - er ba - by

yeah yeah yeah yeah.

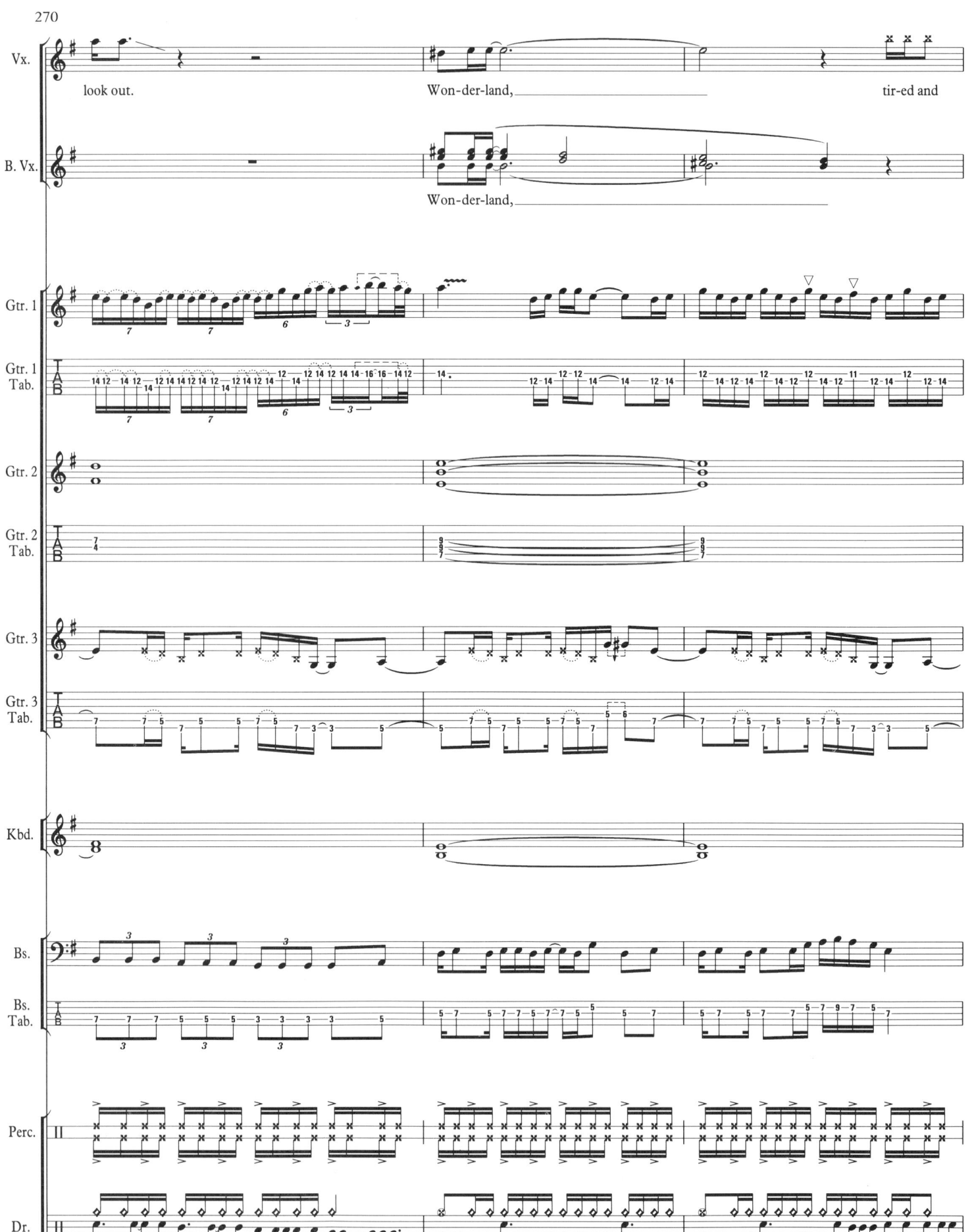

Vx.

look out.   Won-der-land,   tir-ed and

B. Vx.

Won-der-land,

tir-ed and   cheat - ed. _____

Talk a - bout the

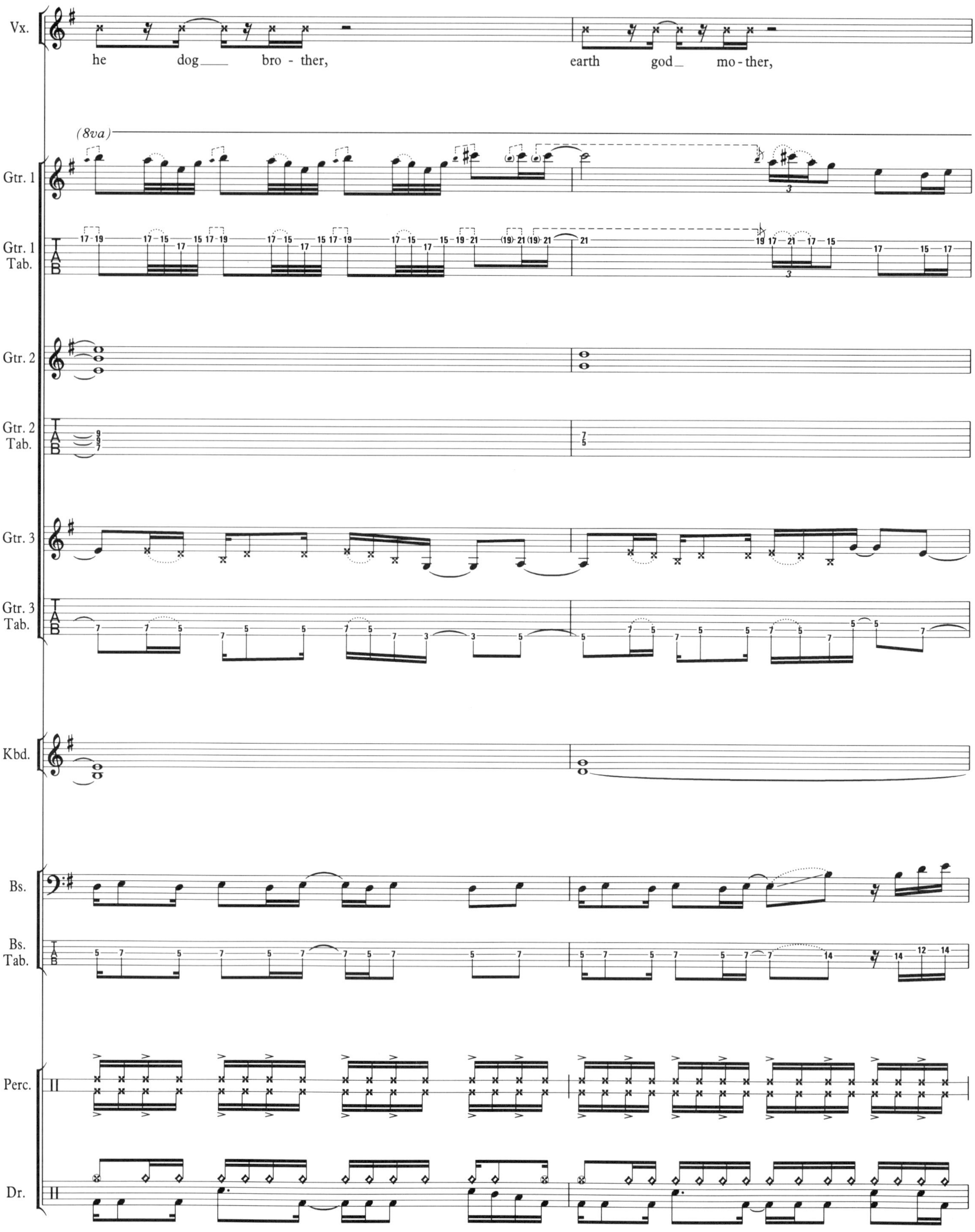
Vx.
he dog bro - ther,
earth god mo - ther,
(8va)
Gtr. 1
Gtr. 1 Tab.
Gtr. 2
Gtr. 2 Tab.
Gtr. 3
Gtr. 3 Tab.
Kbd.
Bs.
Bs. Tab.
Perc.
Dr.

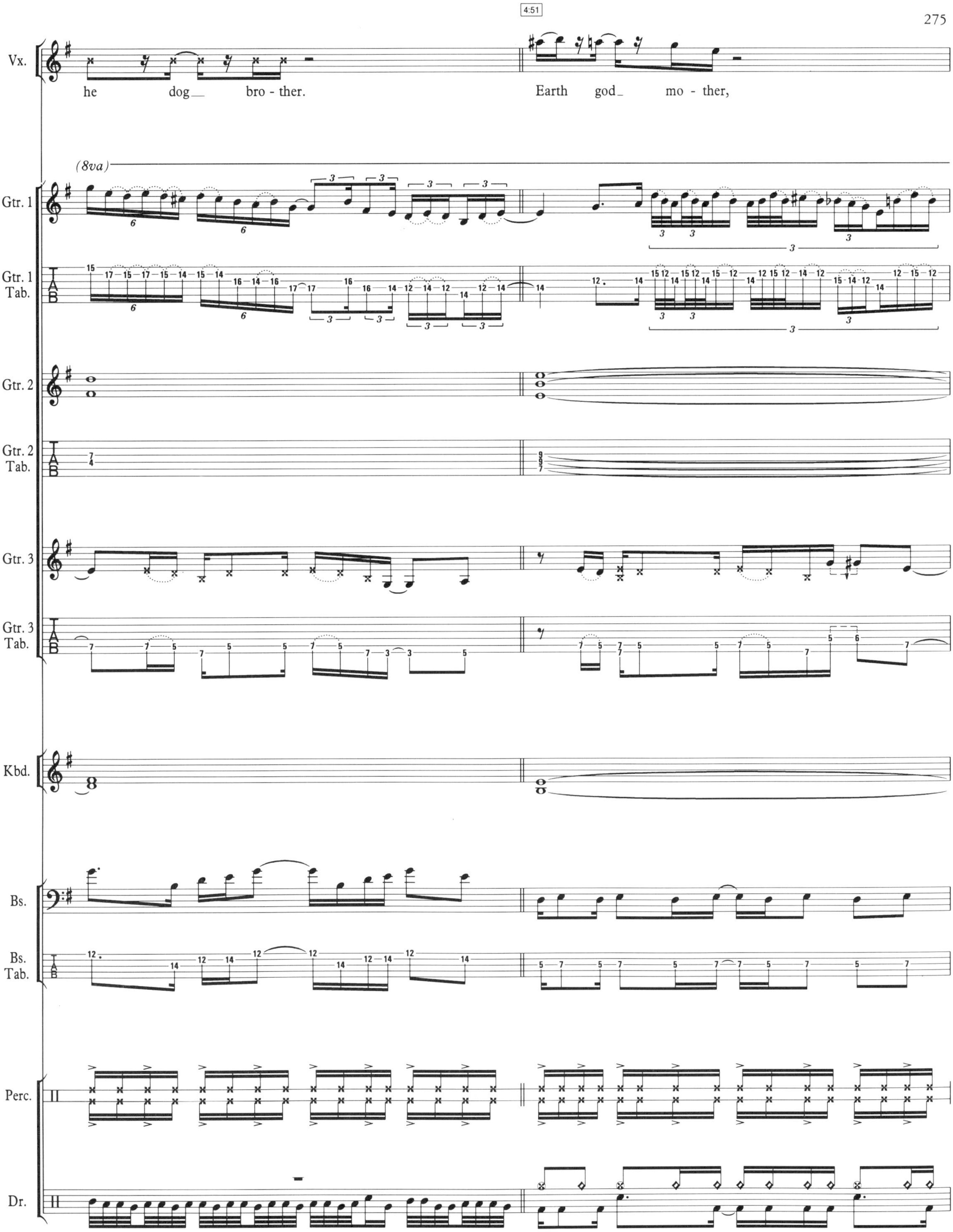
4:51
Vx.
he dog_ bro - ther.
Earth god_ mo - ther,
(8va)
Gtr. 1
Gtr. 1 Tab.
Gtr. 2
Gtr. 2 Tab.
Gtr. 3
Gtr. 3 Tab.
Kbd.
Bs.
Bs. Tab.
Perc.
Dr.

276

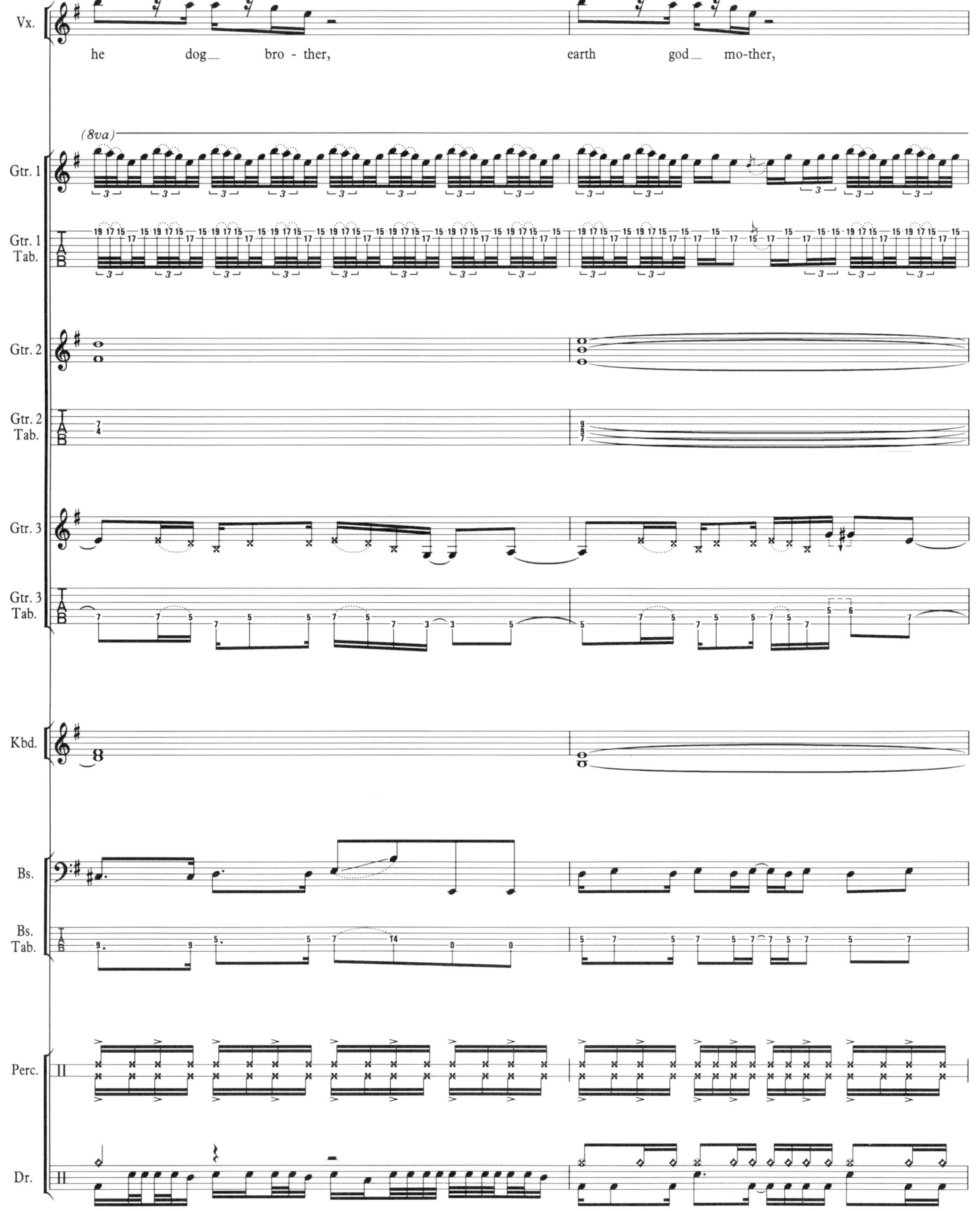

he   dog____ bro - ther,   earth god__ mo-ther.

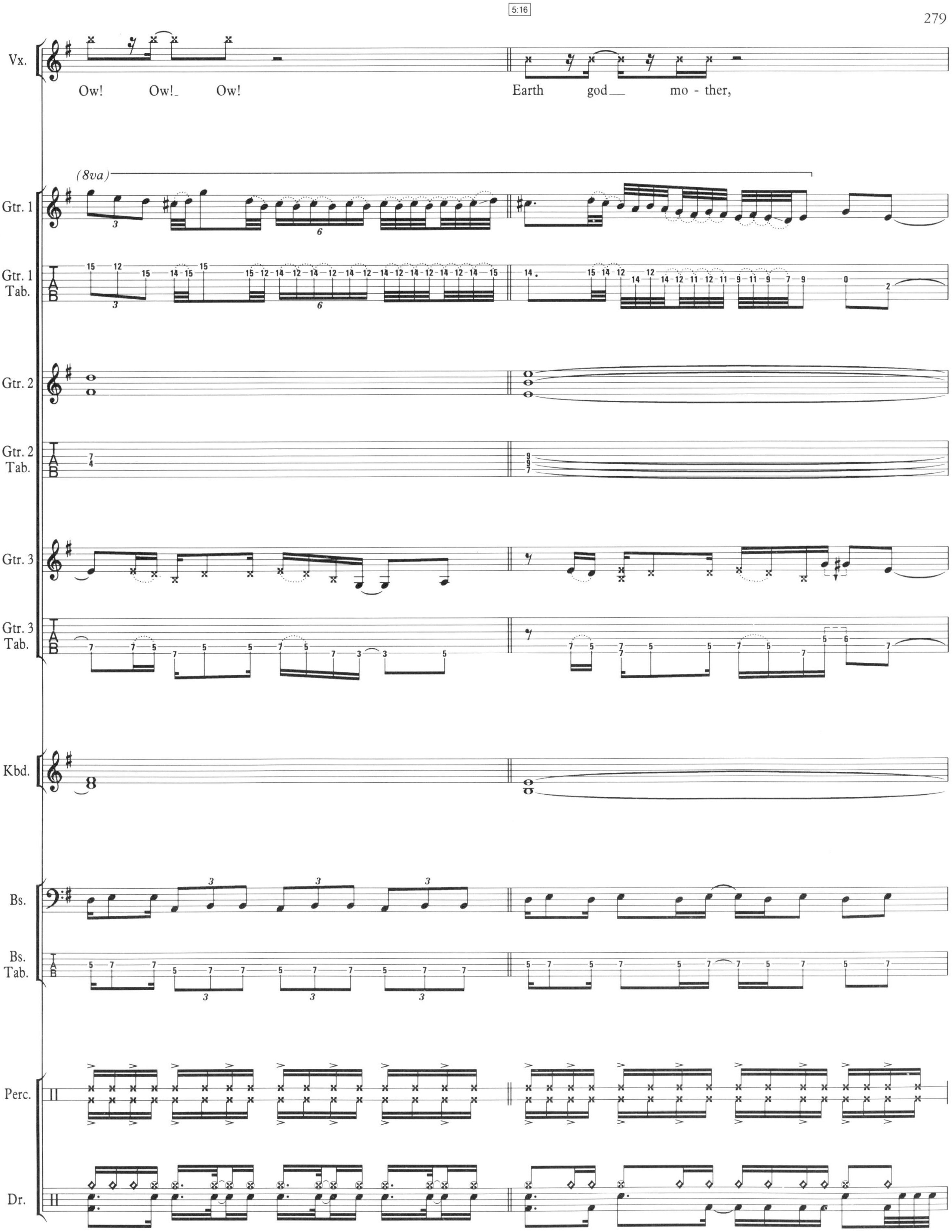
5:16
Vx.
Ow! Ow! Ow!
Earth god mo - ther,
(8va)
Gtr. 1
Gtr. 1 Tab.
Gtr. 2
Gtr. 2 Tab.
Gtr. 3
Gtr. 3 Tab.
Kbd.
Bs.
Bs. Tab.
Perc.
Dr.

284

Vx.

earth god mo-ther,   he dog bro-ther.

Gtr. 1

(8va)

Gtr. 1
Tab.

Gtr. 2

Gtr. 2
Tab.

Gtr. 3

Gtr. 3
Tab.

Kbd.

Bs.

Bs.
Tab.

Perc.

Dr.

Printed in England
Panda Press · Haverhill · Suffolk • 10/92